A MONK OF THE EASTERN CHURCH
ARCHIMANDRITE LEV GILLET

THE JESUS PRAYER

Revised edition with a foreword

by

KALLISTOS WARE
BISHOP OF DIOKLEIA

ST. VLADIMIR'S SEMINARY PRESS
CRESTWOOD, NEW YORK 10707
1987

Library of Congress Cataloging-in-Publication Data

Gillet, Lev
   The Jesus Prayer.

   Translation of: La Prière de Jésus.
   Bibliography: p.
   Includes index.
   1. Jesus prayer. I. Ware, Kallistos, 1934-
II. Title.
BT590.J28G5413   1987   242   86-33916
ISBN 0-88141-013-6

Originally published in French under the title
La Prière de Jésus
by Editions de Chevetogne, Belgium

THE JESUS PRAYER

PRINTED IN THE UNITED STATES OF AMERICA
BY
COSMOS PRINTING ASSOCIATES
NEW YORK, NY

CONTENTS

FOREWORD

"To pronounce the name of Jesus in a holy way is an all-sufficient and surpassing aim for any human life. . . . We are to call to mind Jesus Christ until the name of the Lord penetrates our heart, descends to its very depths. . . . The name of Jesus, once it has become the center of our life, brings everything together."[1]

So writes the "Monk of the Eastern Church" in the course of the present work. To those who wonder how such claims can be advanced on behalf of the Jesus Prayer, and how it is that this particular way of praying continues to appeal so powerfully to contemporary Christians, Eastern and Western, Orthodox and non-Orthodox, this short book provides an answer. Starting with the veneration of the Holy Name in the Old and the New Testament, the author traces the gradual development of the Jesus Prayer first in Byzantium and then in the Slav lands. He concludes with practical suggestions for its use today, showing how it is a prayer not only of the past but equally for the twentieth century. Indeed, there are good reasons to believe that the "way of the name", as he calls it, is being followed by more Christians in our own day than ever before—a striking sign of hope in an age of anxiety. Simple yet profound, this book reveals to us the secret of the continuing attraction exercised by the Jesus Prayer. Since its first appearance some thirty-five years ago, it has become a minor "classic" of the spiritual life, and it still remains the best introduction to the subject.

---

[1]See below, pp. 41, 50, 96.

"The Monk of the Eastern Church", Archimandrite Lev
Gillet (1893-1980), was a person greatly loved and admired.
But he was at the same time enigmatic, sometimes disconcerting, with a character full of paradox, easily mis-
interpreted. It is probably too soon to attempt a balanced
assessment of his life and work.[2] Born at Saint Marcellin in
south-eastern France in 1893[3], he received the name Louis at his
baptism. His parents were Roman Catholics, belonging
socially to the middle classes, and his father was a magistrate
in the Grenoble area. From an early age Louis displayed
exceptional intellectual gifts. He embarked on higher studies
in philosophy at Grenoble and Paris immediately before the
outbreak of the first world war. Mobilized in 1914, he was
shortly afterwards wounded and captured by the Germans,
spending more than two years in a prisoner-of-war camp.
His wartime experiences left him with a lasting revulsion
against violence and bloodshed, and in later life he was by
conviction a pacifist. Released from internment in 1917, he
continued his studies at Geneva, working on experimental
psychology and mathematics. During 1917-19 he translated
from German into French Freud's major work *The Interpre-*

---

[2]We eagerly await the biography of Fr Lev that is being prepared by his
disciple Mme Elisabeth Behr-Sigel. Until this is available, the best account is to
be found in the memorial number issued by the French Orthodox journal
Contacts XXXIII, 116 (1981). His ministry as a Roman Catholic in the 1920s,
immediately before he became Orthodox, is well described by his close friend
Dom Olivier Rousseau, "Le 'Moine de l'Eglise d'Orient'," *Irénikon* LIII, 2
(1980), pp. 175-95. On his entry into the Orthodox Church, see E. Behr-Sigel,
"The Concelebrant at Clamart: Lev Gillet in the year 1927-8," *Sobornost
incorporating Eastern Churches Review* 3, no. 1 (1981), pp. 40-52; cf. her
briefer and more general treatment in *St. Vladimir's Theological Quarterly* 24,
3 (1980), pp. 202-8. Consult also the obituaries by Helle Georgiadis in
Sobornost/ECR 2, no. 2 (1980), pp. 79-85, and at greater length in *Chrysostom*
V, 8 (1980), pp. 230-53. But not all would agree with her interpretation of Fr
Lev's position as an Orthodox: see my own letter in *Chrysostom* VI, 1 (1981),
pp. 16-17. See further David Balfour, "Memories of Fr Lev Gillet," *Sobor-
nost/ECR* 4, no. 2 (1982), pp. 203-11. I am indebted to the sympathetic
portrait of Fr Lev given by Constance Babington Smith in her introduction to
a forthcoming collection of his devotional writings.

[3]H. Georgiadis, in *Chrysostom* V, 8, p. 231, gives the date 1892; O.
Rousseau, in *Irénikon* LIII, 2, p. 175, gives 8 August 1893; the memorial issue
of *Contacts* gives both years: 1892 on the cover, 1893 on p. 257.

tation of Dreams. From his psychological studies he retained always a deep understanding of homosexuality, and indeed of sexual questions in general.

In 1920 Louis Gillet's life took a fundamental change of direction. Abandoning a promising academic career, he entered as a novice in the French Benedictine monastery at Farnborough in England. In due course the community sent him for further studies at Sant' Anselmo in Rome. He had by now begun to feel a strong attraction towards the Christian East. His interest in the Slav world seems to have been awakened initially through a friendship with a young Bulgarian woman whom he met shortly before the first world war. Unable to find someone to teach him Bulgarian, he started to learn Russian instead. Cut off from her at the outbreak of hostilities, he was never able to reestablish contact. Perhaps it was partly this personal disappointment that led him to think of becoming a monk. In the German prisoner-of-war camp he had met Russian soldiers whom he had befriended, continuing his study of Russian. Then, during his time as a novice at Farnborough, the monastery had been visited by the great Uniate leader Andrew Szeptycky, Metropolitan of Lvov in Galicia (at that time within Poland).

Finding his "oriental" interests viewed with little sympathy by the monastic authorities at Farnborough, in 1924 he went to Lvov, and here he was professed a monk and ordained deacon and priest by Metropolitan Andrew, receiving the new monastic name of Lev (Leo). Serving for a while as the Metropolitan's private secretary, Hieromonk Lev was profoundly inspired by Szeptycky's brilliant and saintly personality. A pioneer in the movement for Christian unity, the Metropolitan was convinced that reconciliation between Catholics and Orthodox could come about only through mutual respect and love, not through proselytism. He even envisaged the possibility of a "mixed" monastery in Galicia, in which Orthodox monks might live side by side with Catholics, without being required to abandon their Orthodoxy—a revolutionary idea at that time. Fr Lev shared

his Metropolitan's eirenic vision, although with some reservations. Throughout his life he continued to display a fixed
aversion for all forms of ecclesiastical aggression and polemics. He did not believe that reunion could be achieved
through theological confrontation, through controversy and
formal discussions.

By 1927 Fr Lev was back in France, engaged in social
and pastoral work in Nice among the Russian refugees,
many of whom were living in the utmost material misery.
Here he felt increasingly the anomaly of his situation: he
loved and longed to serve the Russian people, he felt himself
one in heart and soul with Russian Orthodoxy, and yet he
was a Roman Catholic priest. To make matters worse, there
was at this moment a basic change of attitude towards ecu-
menical work on the part of Pope Pius XI, who early in 1928
issued the strongly negative encyclical *Mortalium Animos*.
After months of painful uncertainty, on 25 May 1928 Fr Lev
took a decisive step: at Clamart in the outskirts of Paris, he
concelebrated at the Divine Liturgy with the Russian Orthodox bishop in France, Metropolitan Evlogy. He acted
with the knowledge of Szeptycky.

It is not altogether clear how this step was understood by
Metropolitan Evlogy or by Fr Lev himself. One point,
however, is beyond dispute. The usual formalities required
of Roman Catholic converts to Orthodoxy were omitted. Fr
Lev made no abjuration of errors and underwent no rite of
reception, but was simply admitted to eucharistic concelebration and communion. For him this remained always a
point of major significance. He did not regard his action on
25 May 1928 as a repudiation of his Roman Catholic past, as
a "conversion" in the sense of a change of beliefs and a
rupture with his previous life. Believing that there remained
an underlying unity between Rome and Orthodoxy that was
still unbroken, he saw this step as the deepening and ful-
filment, not the rejection, of all his earlier aspirations. As he
wrote at the time to his brother, "I have gone where I
believed that I could find, I will not say another light, but

the same light in a purer form."[4] In another letter, written to his mother, he said that the Orthodox Church "presents the light of Christ in a purer form than do the other Churches."[5] But he never denied the ecclesial reality of the Roman Catholic Church, nor his own continuing unity with Rome on an invisible, spiritual level.

At the same time the concelebration at Clamart did indeed constitute for Fr Lev a new beginning, the end of one period in his life and the commencement of another. "You may now regard yourself as Orthodox," said Metropolitan Evlogy at the time.[6] For the remaining half-century of his life, from the visible and canonical point of view, Fr Lev served solely as a priest of the Orthodox Church. In the autumn of 1928 Metropolitan Evlogy set him in charge of the French-speaking Orthodox parish in Paris, and to this he remained attached until 1938, teaching also at the Theological Institute of Saint-Serge. He was much interested in the ideas of Archpriest Sergei Bulgakov, the Rector of the Institute, translating into French his work *L'Orthodoxie* (Paris, 1932). Charateristically the translator's name is nowhere mentioned in the publication. During these years he formed also a lasting friendship with the lay theologian Paul Evdokimov.

Fr Lev moved in 1938 to Britain, which was to be his permanent home until his death. In the early 1940s he held a research fellowship in the Department of Missions at the Selly Oak Colleges in Birmingham, studying Jewish-Christian relations and writing *Communion in the Messiah* (London, 1942), the longest of his published books. Here he urges that it is not enough for Christians to be moved with compassion towards the Jew as a human being, but that "the Christian is called to recognize the Jew as a brother," and that to help the Jew "means to help the whole of Israel to fulfil the mysterious destiny to which it is called, and which is in-

[4]Quoted in E. Behr-Sigel, *Contacts* XXXIII, 116, p. 278.
[5]*Ibid.*, p. 282.
[6]O. Rousseau, in *Irénikon* LIII, 2, p. 191.

separable from the destiny of the Christian Church itself." In typical fashion Fr Lev writes in his preface, "This is not a 'learned' book." But it is in fact the fruit of wide reading as well as creative thinking, and it still retains its value.

In 1948 Fr Lev was appointed chaplain to the Fellowship of St Alban and St Sergius, a post that he held for the rest of his life. The Fellowship, which is dedicated to the work of Christian unity, and more especially to Anglican-Orthodox *rapprochement*, maintains a centre in London at St Basil's House, 52 Ladbroke Grove. Here Fr Lev lived in a small room, celebrating the Divine Liturgy in the chapel, and taking a full part in the Fellowship's activities—writing for its journal *Sobornost*, speaking at the annual summer conferences and leading retreats for its members. He was not attached to any specific parish in London, and his work for the Fellowship left him free for journeys abroad, to Switzerland, Greece and above all to the Lebanon, where he greatly influenced the Orthodox Youth Movement. When in London he worked each weekday in the Reading Room of the British Museum, which he used to describe as his monastic cloister. Other readers there will recall his familiar figure, small, bowed, slightly birdlike, with a white beard and thick spectacles—sometimes frowning, twitching a little and muttering to himself as he walked alone, but with his whole face illumined by a smile when he paused to greet a friend. In later life Fr Lev was in many ways an urban hermit, with the great metropolis as his desert. When he speaks in *The Jesus Prayer* about invoking the Holy Name on the men and women whom we pass in the street, "recognizing and silently adoring Jesus imprisoned in the sinner, in the criminal, in the prostitute,"[7] we may be sure that this is exactly what he himself did as he wandered alone in the streets of central London. Wherever he was, whether in Nice, Paris or London, he showed a particular tenderness for the suffering, the destitute. the outcast.

Full of years but mentally alert, the "Monk of the Eastern

---

[7]See below, p. 99.

Church" died in his room at St Basil's House on 29 March 1980. In the Orthodox calendar it was the Saturday of the Resurrection of Lazarus, and he had celebrated his last Liturgy on that same morning.

It was during his years at St Basil's House that Fr Lev developed a form of expression that he made peculiarly his own. More and more he chose to limit himself to short, simple meditations on the Gospel. Usually these were first given as talks—perhaps at meetings of the Fellowship of St Alban and St Sergius in England, or else at Geneva or Beirut—and then they were gathered together and published in book form. Seated at a table, with no script or notes before him but only an opened Bible, Fr Lev could in a few sentences create an atmosphere that was altogether distinctive. Economical in his use of words, avoiding tricks of rhetoric, he spoke with the directness and lucidity that come only after deep thought. He was easy to follow, yet never banal. He spoke from his own experience, yet without referring explicitly to himself; with warmth of personal feeling, yet without sentimentality. He was strikingly original, suggesting meanings that had probably never before occurred to his hearers, yet without being far-fetched or whimsical.

What used to impress me most, as I listened to him, was the *freshness* that marked his interpretation of Scripture. He took some familiar saying or incident from the Gospels—Jesus with the rich young man, with the Samaritan woman at the well, with the woman taken in adultery—and, as he commented on the well-known text, it was as if we were listening to the words of the Bible for the first time, as if we were ourselves part of the scene that he was describing. He did not merely comment, he *announced* the Gospel. "I find contentment only in the Gospel," he once wrote to a friend,[8] and this became increasingly manifest as he advanced in years. In the 1920s and the early 1930s, he was attracted

---

[8]Rousseau, in *Irénikon* LIII, 2, p. 190.

primarily by the Russian tradition—by the *iurodivye* or "fools in Christ", by the luminous compassion of St Seraphim, by the prophetic vision of Soloviev, by the theology of *sobornost*. In his writings during the 1940s, such as *Orthodox Spirituality* (London, 1945), the material is largely from Greek Patristic authors. But in the Scriptural meditations of his later years, it was not about Christian Russia that he spoke, nor yet about the Fathers, but simply about Jesus Christ in the Gospels. As he grew older, he grew ever more transparently "evangelical".

The simplicity and freedom evident in the manner that Fr Lev gave his talks—without notes, with only the Bible before him—was apparent also in other aspects of his life. He adopted the way of *kenosis*, reticence, renunciation. Many of his writings were published under the pseudonym "A Monk of the Eastern Church", and for a long time the author's identity remained a closely guarded secret. A monk without a monastery, he yet observed the rule of poverty with a strictness attained by few who live within monastic enclosure. Apart from his clothes, worn and shabby, he had almost no material possessions that he could call his own. Unlike many monastic clergy, he did not accumulate icons, vestments or crosses. There were few papers and documents and virtually no books in his room. So far as I could see, he did not even have copies of the books that he had himself written, and it seems that he never troubled to keep a list of his own published writings. In his detachment he was a true monk.

The same kenotic approach, the same evangelical freedom and radicalism, characterized all his service within the Church. He avoided administrative responsibilities, committees and outward honors. He detested all forms of clericalism, "seminary outlook" and ecclesiastical pomp, and could be sharply ironical about such things. His pastoral ministry was carried out in a discreet, concealed way, through personal conversations and through informal talks delivered usually to small groups. His counsel, which often had a profound influence for good upon the lives of others, was given in a direct fashion that went quickly to the heart of the matter, but that could seem at times almost abrupt. He used to stress the need for what has been called the "sacrament of the present moment." Christ comes in the little things, he insisted; the divine presence is to be found, not so much in extraordinary situations, but in the familiar tasks that we have daily to fulfil. He possessed a special gift as friend and spiritual guide to women, and in his writings on the women of the Gospels—on the Mother of God, on the woman who was a sinner, on St Mary Magdalen in the garden—there is evident a moving, tender sense of the feminine.

Fr Lev's character was a unity full of contrasts. He was meek yet fiery; gentle and compassionate, yet also moody, "difficult", subject to outbursts of anger, sharply indignant at whatever he saw as lies, unfairness or stupidity. A man of broad culture, always an avid reader, he deliberately concealed his learning. Receptive to new ideas in politics, science and philosophy, he was at the same time deeply traditionalist. His life was, in his own phrase, a "guided exodus", an unceasing pilgrimage; he waited upon the Spirit, and taught others to do the same. Yet, along with this openness to the Spirit, he displayed perseverance, consistency, continuity. In his pastoral work he was sensitive yet rigorous, never blurring the exacting demands made upon us by what he termed "love without limits". An attentive listener, at the full disposition of each visitor, he still remained a "cat that walked by himself"—at home with the other, while never ceasing to be true to his own self.

He loved the Orthodox Church, but was not blind to its shortcomings. "O strange Orthodox Church," he once said, "so poor and so weak. . .at the same time so traditional and yet so free, so archaic and yet so alive, so ritualistic and yet so personally mystical, Church where the pearl of great price of the Gospel is preciously preserved, sometimes beneath a layer of dust. . .Church that has so often proved incapable of acting, yet which knows, as does no other, how to sing the joy of Easter."[9]

---

[9]Homily given on the first anniversary of the death of Msgr Irénée

Beyond the bounds of Orthodoxy, he maintained spiritual links not only with Roman Catholics and Anglicans, but with the French Protestant congregation in London, with Pentecostalists and with Quakers; and, outside Christianity, with Jews and Muslims, with Hindus and Buddhists. Like the Fourth Evangelist and like the Logos theologians of the second century, he believed that the true light, the light of Christ, "enlightens everyone born into the world" (Jn 1:5). His was a universality without relativism. In his quest for unity, he was always seeking to build bridges between separated worlds; not that he favored in any way an ecletic, syncretistic amalgam of religions, but he valued spiritual authenticity wherever it might be found. Wide-ranging contacts were possible for him, precisely because he was himself firmly anchored in the Church, and so could freely recognize the presence of Christ and the movement of the Holy Spirit in *every* person.

The work here issued in a revised English edition was originally published in French as a series of articles in *Irénikon*, the periodical of the Benedictine Monastery of Chevetogne in Belgium (previously at Amay), with which Fr Lev was closely bound through personal friendship, although he had never actually been a member of it. Chapters I-V appeared in *Irénikon* XX (1947), pp. 249-73 and 381-421, and chapter VI in *Irénikon* XXV (1952), pp. 371-82. Chapters I-V, with the two appendices, were issued in book form by the Monastery of Chevetogne in 1951 under the title *La Prière de Jésus*. In 1959 the work was reissued in a revised and expanded form, now including chapter VI: on the title page this is described as the third edition, but I have failed to discover when the second edition appeared (perhaps there never was a second edition). A fourth edition, extensively revised, was published in 1963, and this was used for the first English edition, *The Prayer of Jesus*, translated anonymously by "A Monk of the

---

Winnaert (1938), in Vincent Bourne, *La Queste de Vérité' Irénée Winnaert* (Geneva, 1966), p. 335.

Western Church (Desclée & Cie, Tournai, 1967). A fifth French edition, once more with various modifications, appeared in 1974 in the series *Livre de Vie* (27 rue Jacob, Paris VIe), and this has formed the basis of the present revised English version.

In this, the second English edition, the translation has been thoroughly reworked; I have found it necessary to make changes in almost every paragraph, and often in every sentence. Very occasionally, when I detected a minor factual inaccuracy in the original concerning dating, ascription of authorship or the like, I have ventured to adjust the text; but I trust that nowhere have I altered any value judgement or theological view expressed by Fr Lev. In the footnotes bibliographical references have been brought up to date wherever possible; additional material for which I am responsible is contained within square brackets. I am also responsible for the final section on "Further Reading."

What are the dominant characteristics of Fr Lev's approach to the Jesus Prayer? One of the most impressive features is the warmth of feeling with which he speaks, the evident love for the living person of Christ by which he is inspired. This is particularly apparent in the final chapter, but the same affective, personal note can be heard at many points in the earlier parts of his book, as for example in his explanation of the term "mercy" (pp. 70-71). For the "Monk of the Eastern Church" the Jesus Prayer is not a technique but an act of love. It expresses a direct relationship between persons. When saying the Jesus Prayer, he tells us, we are not to think about the fact we are invoking the name, about the "method" of prayer that we are using and its possible effects; we are to think simply and solely of Jesus himself.

Throughout his teaching on the Prayer Fr Lev shows great sobriety and discretion. While believing that the Prayer does indeed possess a special power to "simplify and unify our spiritual life" (p. 96), he is careful not to make exaggerated claims on its behalf. The name of Jesus is not a talisman or "magical formula", he says, "for no one

can use this name effectively if he does not have an inner
relationship with Jesus himself" (p. 27). The Jesus Prayer is
not to be isolated, but presupposes the total living of the
Christian life in all its varied forms—communal prayer,
receiving of the sacraments, Scripture reading, acts of personal service and compassion: "The Jesus Prayer is a book
to be opened and read only in an evangelical spirit of
humble love and self-giving" (p. 76). In particular it does
not render unnecessary the Cross-bearing to which every
baptized Christian is committed: "Let us not imagine that
the invocation of the name is a 'short-cut' that dispenses us
from ascetic purification" (p. 96).

Some exponents talk as if the Jesus Prayer and "Orthodox spirituality" were more or less interchangeable
equivalents, but Fr Lev makes no such sweeping statements. He respects the full diversity and freedom in our
human approach to God. The "way of the name" is open
to all, but no one is compelled to adopt it, and it enjoys no
exclusive monopoly: "We should not cry out with an ill-
informed fervor, 'It is the best prayer,' much less, 'It is the
only prayer'" (p. 95). Only for those who have received "a
very special vocation" will the Jesus Prayer become "*the*
method around which their whole interior life is organized"
(p. 95).

Fr Lev wisely cautions us against the perils of emo-
tionalism, of inner violence, in this as in other ways of
praying: "It would be a mistake to 'force' this prayer, to
raise our voice inwardly, to try to induce intensity and
emotion. . . . Let us banish all spiritual sensuality" (p. 94).
He has some helpful counsel here about periods of dryness
in prayer: perhaps the times when we have felt no emo-
tional consolation as we prayed are particularly precious in
God's sight (pp. 94-95). We are to seek, not "experiences",
but only Jesus Christ.

Discussing the controversial "physical technique" sometimes associated with the Jesus Prayer, the "Monk" takes
great care to insist that this is no more than an accessory,

beneficial perhaps to some, but in no sense obligatory upon all: "The invocation of the name of Jesus is sufficient by itself. Its best supports are of a spiritual and moral order. Moreover, none of the followers of the Athonite technique has ever maintained that this technique is essential to the Jesus Prayer. . . . The Jesus Prayer confers upon us freedom from everything except Jesus himself" (p. 74). Fr Lev emphasizes also the importance of obedience, of spiritual direction given by an experienced guide. This is desirable for all who use the Jesus Prayer, and in the case of anyone proposing to adopt the "physical technique" it is indispensable.

In all this Fr Lev faithfully reflects the classic teaching on the Jesus Prayer. There are, however, three points where his view of the Prayer reflects a personal standpoint of his own, not shared today by most others who treat the subject. First, in his judgement the Jesus Prayer consisted originally in the name "Jesus" recited on its own, not in some more developed formula such as "Lord Jesus Christ, Son of God, have mercy on me," or the like. "The oldest, the simplest, and in our opinion the easiest formula," he writes, "is the word 'Jesus' used alone" (p. 93); reciting the name on its own, we can recover a "primitive freedom", less in evidence during the later evolution of the Prayer (p. 71). Accordingly, in his chapter on the practical use of the Prayer Fr Lev has in view the employment simply of the name "Jesus", although in fact almost everything that he has to say is applicable equally to the developed formula in its different variants.

The Jesuit scholar Fr Irénée Hausherr disagrees here with the "Monk of the Eastern Church". "The Jesus Prayer," he writes in his great study *Noms du Christ et voies d'oraison*, "did not commence with the name of Jesus. It had its beginnings in *penthos*, in mourning, in sorrow for sin. . . . For the developed formula, at least as regards its substance, we have many pages of documentary evidence; for the use of the name alone we have very few witnesses; in the formal sense, we have nothing at all."[10] In Fr Hausherr's view the "developed formula" represents not so much an expansion as an abbreviation, a concentration into one short phrase of the quintessence of the monastic spirituality of *penthos*.

In support of Fr Lev, it is possible to quote certain examples through the centuries in which the name "Jesus" is used alone (see below, pp. 62, 83). But it has to be admitted that the bulk of the evidence favors Fr Hausherr. "Monologic" prayer—prayer of a single *logos*—generally means prayer of a single phrase, not just of a single word. St Diadochus of Photike, the earliest author to give a specific formula, mentions not "Jesus" alone but "Lord Jesus", possibly followed by other words (p. 37). A few years later, St Barsanuphius and St John of Gaza (pp. 37-38) give a variety of formulae, all of them containing several words, never "Jesus" on its own. But, whatever the true facts about the historical development of the Prayer— and gaps in the evidence mean that no final conclusion is possible—Fr Lev is fully entitled to recommend to Christians of our own day the use of the Holy Name by itself; and this was in fact customary in the West during the Middle Ages. Some may find the name, when invoked on its own, almost too powerful, too intense, and they will prefer to "dilute" it with other words. But many will agree with Fr Lev that "Jesus" alone is indeed "the simplest and. . . the easiest formula". In this, as in all aspects of the life of prayer, personal diversity may exist.

Secondly, when recounting the development of the Jesus Prayer, Fr Lev distinguishes between a "Sinaite" stage (fifth to seventh century) and an "Athonite" stage (fourteenth century onwards). This conception of "Sinaite spirituality" was taken over by Fr Lev from an early work by Fr Hausherr, *La méthode d'oraison hésychaste* (Rome, 1927), but in his later writings from 1934 onwards the learned Jesuit abandoned the idea. The early evolution of the Jesus Prayer,

---

[10]*Noms du Christ* (Rome, 1960), p. 118; Eng. trans., *The Name of Jesus* (Kalamazoo, 1978), p. 104.

so he maintains in *Noms du Christ*, is not connected in any decisive fashion with Sinai, and the very notion of a specifically "Sinaite" stage is artificial and misleading (see below, p. 36, note 1). Once more it must be conceded that the evidence on the whole favors Fr Hausherr. The sources of the Jesus Prayer lie in the spirituality of the Desert Fathers of Egypt (see pp. 30-31), while the earlist explicit witnesses are scattered over a wide area—Asia Minor (Nilus), northern Greece (Diadochus), and Palestine (Barsanuphius and John, Dorotheus). Climacus, Hesychius and Philotheus do indeed constitute a distinctively "Sinaite" school, but they are not the earliest witnesses to the Jesus Prayer. Most specialists therefore prefer to follow Fr Hausherr, and now avoid the term "Sinaite spirituality", except when applying it in a restricted manner to these three authors. Fr Lev, however, is himself careful to point out that he is not employing the word "Sinaite" in a narrowly geographical sense (p. 35).

Thirdly and finally, Fr Lev seems less than just in what he writes concerning St Gregory Palamas and the Hesychast controversy (pp. 58-61). He is correct in saying that "Gregory did not discuss the Jesus Prayer as a topic on its own," and so has only a limited place in a study devoted specially to the invocation of the name. It is also regrettably true that much of what Palamas wrote is marked by a sharply polemical tone that Christians today on the whole find unattractive (the same, however, has to be said of many earlier Fathers). Yet St Gregory Palamas possesses a crucial significance for Orthodox theology and spirituality that the "Monk" has failed to make clear. His treatment of the great Hesychast theologian is altogether insufficient. Here Fr Lev has allowed his lifelong distaste for religious controversy to impair his judgement.

As a whole, however, *The Jesus Prayer* is a work remarkable for its balance, moderation and generosity. Fr Lev wrote this, as indeed he wrote all his books, with a practical aim in view: not to transmit historical information, but to lead others to pray, to kindle in their hearts a more ardent love for Jesus Christ. *The Jesus Prayer* since its first publication has done exactly that, as I know from my own experience and from what others have told me. At the end of his last chapter the "Monk" tells us of the "special blessing" received by those who love the name of Jesus. May his book, issued now in a revised form, continue to initiate more and more Christians into this way of praying that is ancient yet always new, helping them to share in the "special blessing" of which he speaks. "I will wait upon thy name" (Ps 52:9).

† BISHOP KALLISTOS OF DIOKLEIA

INTRODUCTION

The history of the "Jesus Prayer"—a technical term in Byzantine spirituality which designates the invocation of the name Jesus, whether alone or inserted into a more or less extended formula—has yet to be recounted in a comprehensive way, although there are various studies on points of detail. We make no claim here to provide an exhaustive historical account; we should only like to indicate certain stages in the development of the Prayer. The subject has an interest that is more than purely historical. While the practice of the Prayer goes back to early times, it still remains very much alive today in the Christian East. It is not generally mentioned in standard treatises on the "ways of prayer," and yet it is more ancient and more widespread than the methods analyzed in the classic manuals. A Romanian writer, N. Crainic, has written that the Jesus Prayer is the "heart of Orthodoxy."[1] The Uniates also use it; Latins have taken an interest in it; there are Anglicans and Protestants of our day who fervently follow this method of prayer; it is our common patrimony. More than a private devotion, it borders on the realm of liturgy and even penetrates it. Its implications and possibilities deserve careful attention. May this publication help to attract even a few persons to the practice of it.

We have learned with joy that the earlier editions of our small work have borne fruit. The book, we are told, has helped some souls to learn better the treasures that are contained in the Most Sweet Name of the Savior. *Non nobis, Domine, sed nomini tuo. . . .*

---

[1] N. Crainic, "Das Jesusgebet," an article translated from the Romanian by W. Biemel in *Zeitschrift für Kirchengeschichte* 60 (1941), pp. 341-53. The article is conspicuously lacking in critical judgment: the author attributes the invention of the Jesus Prayer to the Blessed Virgin Mary. This might be true in some mystical sense, but cannot be affirmed as a fact of history.

CHAPTER I

THE INVOCATION OF THE NAME OF JESUS
IN SCRIPTURE
AND THE PATRISTIC TRADITION

The Jesus Prayer has its immediate roots in the New Testament, but its distant roots reach down into the Old Covenant. It is derived, to a certain extent, from the attitude which the Hebrew Bible adopts towards God's name. For the Hebrews the name of Yahweh, in common with his word, was a kind of entity detachable from the divine person, a greatness existing in itself, alongside this person. Thus the angel is considered as the bearer of the name (Ex 23:21) and the prophet sees this name coming from afar (Is 30:27). If the divine name is invoked upon a country or a person, it belongs henceforth to Yahweh; it becomes strictly his and enters into intimate relations with him (Gn 48:16; Dt 28:10; Am 9:12). The name abides in the temple (1 Kgs 8:29). The name is a guide in man's life and in his service of God (Mi 4:5). Throughout the Psalms, the divine name appears as a refuge, a power that comes to our aid, an object of worship.

The veneration of the divine name occurs among nations other than Israel. It is found again and again among the Mandeans, and also in the cult of Isis and Astarte. The name of the divinity plays an important role in the religion of primitive people; for them the name is something real, substantial, a fragment of the being or person named, a kind of "double."[1] But only a superficial criticism would conclude, in the light of these similarities, that the Biblical

---

[1]G. Berguer, "La puissance du nom " (Communication at the Sixth International Congress of the History of Religions, Brussels, 1935, reproduced in *Archives de psychologie de la Suisse romande*, vol. 25, 1936).

attitude toward the name of God is no more than a survival from prerational ways of thinking. The use of the name of Yahweh in the Old Testament does not stem from magic; it is not an arbitrary formula used to produce certain effects. It is true that the Hebrew mentality, like that of the Semites, is especially attached to the name; but this psychological tendency corresponds to an objective, divine disclosure, existing primarily on the spiritual level. On the one hand the name of Yahweh is a revelation of his person, an expression of the divine essence. On the other hand, this revelation, this new phase in the knowledge of the divinity, indicates man's entry into a new, personal, practical relationship with God. To learn who and what he is, is to learn also how one must act.[2]

The Rabbinical tradition contributes further to the veneration of the divine name. We know that out of respect the name of Yahweh, the *tetragrammaton*, was never invoked except by the high priest on the day of Yom Kippur;[3] the word Adonai was substituted for it. The very term by which the divine name was designated, *shem ha-mephorash*, that is to say, the "ineffable name," has a curious history. Literally this term connotes the very opposite of ineffable, for originally it meant "name clearly pronounced." But, little by little, as a veil of adoration covered the divine name, the same term which had signified that the name was openly proclaimed began to indicate that the name had become unutterable. The semantic evolution of a word marks here the development of a cult.

The Cabbalists attached special importance to the divine name. It cannot be denied that some of them fell into superstitions concerning the use of letters, numbers and formulas; and yet, in all fairness, we must recognize that the Cabbala in its essence was not a kind of magic but a method both of spiritual exegesis and of spiritual life.

---

[2]F. Giesebrecht, *Die alttestamentliche Schätzung des Gottesnamens und ihre religionsgeschichtliche Grundlage* (Konigsberg i Pr., 1901); L. Brockington, "The Hebrew Conception of Personality in Relation to the Knowledge of God," in *The Journal of Theological Studies* 47 (1946), pp. 1-11.

[3]Talmud, *Yoma* 6, 2.

Jewish tradition uses the term *baal shem*, "master of the name," without magical connotations, to designate a particular person credited with possessing effective prayer and a certain power before God. It is a title applied, for example, to Benjamin ben Zara in the 11th century, and to Israel ben Eliezer in the 18th—the saintly Jew who founded the great modern school of mysticism known as Hassidism —and, closer to our own time, to Eli Gutmacher in the 19th century.

Finally we should note the importance, both in ancient as well as in contemporary Jewish spirituality, of the two conceptions *kiddush hash-shem*, "sanctification of the name," and *hillul hash-shem*, "profanation of the name." The expression "sanctification of the name" does not signify simply honor or praise rendered to God's name. It is a technical term already in use in the first century with a very strong meaning: to sanctify the name is to bear testimony to God at the risk of one's own life, it is to glorify God, if need be, even to the shedding of blood. The sanctification of the name became almost synonymous with martyrdom. The Maccabees were considered as the sanctifiers *par excellence* of the divine name. The Jewish notion of *kiddush hash-shem* sheds particular light on the first request in the Lord's Prayer.[4]

*

* *

The angel announced to Mary that her son would be called Jesus, for he would save men from their sins (Mt 1:21; cf. Lk 1:13). The name Ἰησοῦς is the Greek tran-

---

[4]On *kiddush hash-shem* and *hillul hash-shem*, cf. Kaufmann Kohler, *Jewish Theology systematically and historically considered* (New York, 1928), pp. 348ff. More generally, A. Marmorstein, *The Old Rabbinic Doctrine of God*, I: *The Names and Attributes of God* (London, 1927), and the article *God (Name of)*, in *Universal Jewish Encyclopedia*, vol. 5 (New York, 1941).

[On the veneration of the name in the Bible, see also H. Bietenhard,

scription of the Hebrew *Yeshua* (Jesus), which is itself
identical with *Yehoshua* (Joshua). The first of these two
Hebrew words is a contraction of the second, intended to
avoid the sequence of the vowels *o* and *u* which was
repugnant to Jewish ears. The meaning of the name *Yeshua*,
while clear in a general sense, is difficult to establish with
any strict precision. The translation "savior" is more or less
correct; more exactly the name signifies "salvation of
Yahweh" or "Yahweh is salvation."[5] Hence the ancient adage
nomen est omen—the name expresses in a certain way the
person and his destiny—applies to the angel's Annunciation
concerning the name of the child.

Three texts from the New Testament are of special
importance for the veneration of the name of Jesus. First of
all (following what we believe to be the chronological
order) there is St Paul's great text: "God has given him a
name which is above all names, that at the name of Jesus
every knee should bow, of those that are in heaven, on
earth, and under the earth" (Phil 2:9-10). Next we have the
solemn declaration from the Acts of the Apostles: "There is
no other name under heaven given to men whereby we
must be saved" (Acts 4:12). And finally in the Fourth
Gospel we have the secret which Jesus reveals to his disciples: "Hitherto you have not asked anything in my name.
. . Whatever you ask the Father in my name, he will give it
you" (Jn 16:23-24).

The New Testament references to the name of Jesus are
too numerous for us to pause at each one of them; but
every student, with the help of a concordance, could do so

"'Ονομα," in G. Kittel and G. Friedrich, *Theological Dictionary of the New
Testament*, translated by G.W. Bromiley, vol. 5 (Grand Rapids, 1968), pp. 242-81;
J. Pedersen, *Israel*, vol. 1 (London/Copenhagen, 1926), pp. 245-59; G. von Rad,
Old Testament Theology (Edinburgh/London, 1962-5), vol. 1, pp. 179-87; vol. 2,
pp. 80-85. But note the more sceptical approach in J. Barr, "The Symbolism of
Names in the Old Testament," in *Bulletin of the John Rylands Library* 52, 1
(1969), pp. 11-29; A.C. Thiselton, "The Supposed Power of Words in the Biblical
Writings," in *The Journal of Theological Studies* 25 (1974), pp. 283-99.]

[5]A. Deissmann, "The Name of Jesus," in *Mysterium Christi. Christological
Studies by British and German Theologians*, edited by G.K.A. Bell and D.A.
Deissmann (London, 1930), pp. 3-27.

with great profit. The Apocalypse furnishes an especially rich harvest. But it is above all the Acts of the Apostles which could be called the book of the name of Jesus. "In the name of Jesus" the good news is preached, converts believe, baptism is conferred, cures and other "signs" are accomplished, lives are risked and given.[6] What is involved in this insistence on the name of Jesus is not just the employment of a magical formula, for no one can use this name effectively if he does not have an inner relationship with Jesus himself.

Unfortunately the English expression "in the name of," like the Latin *in nomine,* is powerless to render the rich complexity of the Greek terms. In Latin and English the phrase "in the name of Jesus" is more or less synonymous with "by the authority of Jesus"; "in the name of. . ." becomes "by virtue of." This is to impoverish the New Testament Greek, stripping it of both its realism and its nuances. The Greek text, when referring to the name of Jesus, uses three formulas: ἐπὶ τῷ ὀνόματι, εἰς τὸ ὄνομα, ἐν τῷ ὀνόματι. These three formulas are not equivalent, but each one expresses a special attitude toward the name. In ἐπὶ τῷ ὀνόματι, one leans "on" the name; it is the foundation on which one builds, the *terminus a quo,* the point of departure toward a subsequent action, the start of a new advance. In εἰς τὸ ὄνομα, there is a movement "toward" the name, a dynamic relationship of finality which sees the name as the goal to be attained, the *terminus ad quem.* In ἐν τῷ ὀνόματι, the attitude is static; it expresses the repose which follows the attainment of the goal and a certain interiorization or immanence; our spirit is transported "into" the name, within the name, it is united to the name and makes its abode there. 'Εν τῷ ὀνόματι corresponds to the Hebrew *be-shem,* εἰς τὸ ὄνομα to the Hebrew *le-shem.*

---

[6]W. Heitmüller, *"'Im Namen Jesu." Eine sprach- und religionsgeschichtliche Untersuchung zum Neuen Testament, speziell zur altchristlichen Taufe,* in W. Bousset and H. Gunkel, *Forschungen zur Religion und Literatur des Alten und Neuen Testaments* (Göttingen, 1903), I. Bd., 2. Heft. While paying tribute to the wealth of material gathered together in this work, we absolutely reject Heitmüller's conclusions.

Father Ferdinand Prat has clearly indicated[7] the differences between these three formulas, which could provide us with the plan of an entire way of prayer centering around the name of Jesus.

*

* *

The most ancient Patristic references to the name of Jesus are found in the *Shepherd* of Hermas (first half of the 2nd century). Hermas says that for someone "to bear the name of Son of God" is "to lay aside mortality and to assume life."[8] He also says that "no one can enter the Kingdom of God except through the name of his Son."[9] He speaks of "those who have suffered for the name of the Son."[10] Are we to see in this only allusions to baptism and martyrdom, or the first beginnings of a theology of the name? This second hypothesis would seem to be suggested by another statement from Hermas: "The name of the Son of God is great and boundless, and it is this that upholds the entire world."[11] The Byzantine mystics who in the Middle Ages propagated the Jesus Prayer would joyfully have endorsed this statement. If we read carefully the few lines which follow it and the chapter preceding that from which it is taken, we are likely to find somewhat confusing the way in which the name of the Son and the names of virgins, powers and stones are all mixed together. But we gain the impression that for Hermas the name is something very real, having an objective and ontological value.

Origen in the 3rd century did not discuss the theology of the name, even though Alexandrian speculation could

---

[7]*Jésus-Christ, sa vie, sa doctrine, son oeuvre* (Paris, 1933), vol. II, note Z, pp. 564-567.

[8]*Shepherd*, Book III, Similitude IX, 16.

[9]*Ibid.*, 12.

[10]*Ibid.*, 28.

[11]*Ibid.*, 14.

have found here much food for thought. But he remarks that in his time the name of Jesus produces the same effects as in the apostolic age: "Even today the name of Jesus frees people from mental distraction, puts devils to flight, cures the sick; it infuses a wonderful meekness and tranquility of character, love for mankind, and kindness and gentleness. . . ."[12] One might have expected the great Greek theologians of the 4th and 5th centuries to meditate deeply on the name of Jesus. But as a matter of fact neither Athanasius, nor the Cappadocians, nor Chrysostom, nor Cyril of Alexandria gave special attention to the significance of names. If any of them mentions the matter, it is in an incidental way, sometimes as a detail in a biography that they are writing, but it is not a theme developed in their teaching. The Greek Fathers who influenced the growth of devotion to the name are not dogmatic theologians but stand more or less outside the great speculative currents, being concerned with questions of the inner life.

Turning to the Latin West, we find that St Ambrose (†397) devoted much personal reflection to the name of Jesus. According to him, this name was contained in Israel like perfume in a closed vessel. Now the vessel has been opened and the perfume has spread everywhere. There has been a real "outpouring of this name," an outpouring or overflowing of grace; as Ambrose puts it, *ex abundantia superfluit quidquid effunditur*.[13]

St Paulinus of Nola (354-431) wrote a poem on the name of Christ: this name is "nectar in the mouth, honey on the tongue. . ."; it is "a living ambrosia. . .if you have tasted it but once, you cannot endure to be parted from it"; it is "for the eyes a serene light, in the ears the sound of life."[14] It was perhaps this poem which, many years later,

---

[12]*Contra Celsum*, I, 67. [On the significance of the name as rendering present the person, see Origen, *On Prayer* XXIV, 2, commenting on the clause "Hallowed be Thy name" in the Lord's Prayer: "A name is a short and comprehensive title that brings before us the distinctive character of the thing named." Origen held that names exist, not just "by convention," but "by nature": *Exhortation to Martyrdom* 46; *Contra Celsum* V, 45.]

[13]*De Spiritu Sancto*, I, VIII, 96 (*PL* 16, col. 727D).

[14]*PL* 61, col. 741A.

inspired St Bernard. Pope St Damasus (366-84) also wrote
two acrostic poems on the name of Jesus.[15] St Caesarius
of Arles (470-542) connected the name of Jesus with the
brazen serpent: *videte nomen Dei vestri quantum prodesse
possit in gratia quod tantum profuit in figura,* "Consider
how much the name of your God can profit you in grace
when figuratively its power was already so great."[16] St
Augustine hardly ever spoke of the name of Jesus. One
day, however, he came across a text from Habakkuk which
the Latin rendered thus, *Gaudebo in Deo salutari meo,* "I
will rejoice in God my salvation." Augustine knew that
certain other Latin manuscripts gave the reading *Gaudebo
in Deo Jesu meo,* "I will rejoice in God my Jesus." The
equivalence in meaning between the Latin *salutaris* or *salvator*
and the Hebrew *Yeshua* could justify to some extent this
alternative reading. And so Augustine wrote these words
which shed an unexpected light on his feelings: "The reading
in certain manuscripts, 'I will rejoice in God my Jesus,' seems
to me better than that in other manuscripts which, seeking to
translate the word [*Yeshua*] into Latin, have not retained the
actual name [of Jesus]—the name that is so dear to us, so
sweet to pronounce."[17]

One of Augustine's contemporaries, the historian Paul
Orosius, relates an event which probably occurred about
the year 173. The invocation of the name of Christ by
Christian soldiers of the *Legio XII Fulminata* obtained for
them both rain and victory.[18] That the divine name should
work wonders seemed natural. St Athanasius mentions in
passing that it was enough to invoke the name of Christ to
put devils to flight.[19] St Gregory of Nyssa, in his life of St
Gregory the Wonderworker, says that Gregory terrified the
devils by his invocation of the name of Christ.[20]

The Desert Fathers were well acquainted with the power

[15]*Carmina* IV and V (*PL* 13, cols. 377-8).
[16]*Homilia* 2 (*PL* 67, col. 1047B).
[17]*De civitate Dei* XVIII, 32 (*PL* 41, col. 591).
[18]*Historiarum adversum paganos libri* VII, 15.
[19]*On the Incarnation* 48 (*PG* 25, col. 181B).
[20]*PG* 46, col. 916A.

of the name. St Athanasius reports that St Antony of Egypt (†about 356) exorcised a devil by using the name of the Lord Jesus Christ.[21] St Jerome records the same thing of St Hilarion (†about 371).[22] It does not seem that the Desert Fathers practiced the invocation of the name in an organized way. Among the Apophthegmata of the Fathers collected by Bousset, we find only two, of Syrian origin, on the name of Jesus. It is not much. But these monastic circles prepared the way for the Jesus Prayer in another manner. They gave to their private prayers the form of short aspirations. St Augustine wrote about this to Proba: "They say that the brethren in Egypt offer prayers that are frequent but very brief and suddenly shot forth."[23] These words of Augustine, *orationes. . .quodammodo jaculatas,* have given rise to the expression "ejaculatory prayer." They were swift arrows shot toward the heart of God. The Desert Fathers used the formula *Kyrie eleison* or the verse "O God, come to my aid; O Lord, make haste to help me" (Ps 70:1). It is God who is invoked; there is no special mention of the name of the Son. But suppose that one day this name is associated with ejaculatory prayer, that there is a meeting, a fusion, between name and aspiration—then we shall have the Jesus Prayer.[24]

*

* *

This combination was the work of Hesychasm. Often this term has been given too limited an historical meaning, with the title "Hesychast" restricted to the Byzantine mystics

---

[21]*Life of St Antony* 63 (*PG* 26, col. 933A).

[22]*Life of St Hilarion* 22 (*PL* 23, col. 40A).

[23]*Epist.* CXXX, 20 (*PL* 33, col. 501).

[24]M. Viller and K. Rahner, *Aszese und Mystik in der Väterzeit. Ein Abriss* (Freiburg im Breisgau, 1939), ch. 12, par. 41. [Cf. L. Regnault, "La prière continuelle 'monologistos' dans la littérature apophtegmatique," in *Irénikon* 47 (1947), pp. 467-93.]

of the 14th century, especially those of the Palamite school.
In reality Hesychasm is a spiritual tradition extending from
the 5th to the 18th century.[25] The word *hesychia* was well
established as a technical term in the first half of the 7th
century when St John Climacus devoted a chapter to it in
his treatise *The Ladder.*[26] But from the 5th century this
tradition was already represented by such men as St Nilus
of Ancyra or the Sinaite, St Diadochus of Photike, and St
John the Hesychast whose life was written by Cyril of
Scythopolis.[27] One might consider St Nicodemus of the
Holy Mountain, in the 18th century, as the last spokesman
of historical Hesychasm.

How then is Hesychasm to be defined? The word
hesychia signifies "repose." The Hesychast monastic ideal is
to be understood in terms of its relationship both to the
early Desert Fathers and to the cenobitic monasticism of St
Basil and St Theodore the Studite. Like the primitive
monasticism of the Desert, Hesychasm insists on silence,
withdrawal, and a rigorous separation from the world, almost a severing of all human contacts. But it is less pre-
occupied with ascetic feats than is the Desert; instead it puts
the main emphasis upon prayer, contemplation and mystical life, and—what is new—it pursues specific methods of
praying and seeks to develop a contemplative technique. As
regards Basilian and Studite monasticism, Hesychasm differs
from it in a very definite way. The Basilian and Studite
tradition recommends a moderate degree of cenobitic observance, common life and common prayer; Hesychasm
insists upon individual sanctification in solitude. The first

---

[25]Cf. J. Bois, "Les hésychastes avant le XIVe siècle," in *Echos d'Orient* 5 (1901),
pp. 1-11. See also P. Adnès, "Hésychasme," in *Dictionnaire de Spiritualité* 7 (1968),
cols. 381-99; I. Hausherr, "L'hésychasme. Etude de spiritualité," in *Orientalia
Christiana Periodica* 22 (1956), pp. 5-40, 247-85, reprinted in *Hésychasme et prière
(Orientalia Christiana Analecta* 176: Rome, 1966), pp. 163-237. [Cf. Kallistos Ware,
"Silence in Prayer: the Meaning of *Hesychia*," in Basil Pennington (ed.), *One Yet
Two (Cistercian Studies Series* 29: Kalamazoo, 1976), pp. 22-47.]

[26]*Ladder* 27 (*PG* 88, cols. 1096-1101).

[27]Greek text, ed. E. Schwartz, *Kyrillos von Skythopolis (Texte und Unter-
suchungen* 49, 2: Leipzig, 1939), pp. 201-22; French translation by A.J. Festugière,
Les moines d'Orient III, 2 (Paris, 1963), pp. 13-34.

allows monks on occasion to take part in ecclesiastical or charitable activities; the second advocates a radical separation from the world. The first is especially interested in *praxis*, while the second is concerned with *theoria*.

We shall distinguish in the history of Hesychasm, and consequently in the history of the Jesus Prayer, two very distinct phases: the Sinaite phase and the Athonite phase.

CHAPTER II

THE JESUS PRAYER
IN SINAITE HESYCHASM

It was in 527 that the Emperor Justinian I established on Sinai the famous monastery of St Catherine which, even today, constitutes by itself one of the autocephalous Orthodox Churches. But Christians were living on the peninsula already by the year 400. Bordering on the monastic deserts of Egypt, it offered an ideal location for monasticism. At an early date it became a center of spiritual influence. But when we speak of Sinaite spirituality, it is not to be envisaged as strictly localized. What is meant is the spirituality of which the monasticism of Sinai constitutes a focal point and an example; we have in mind a current of thought and a common tendency, but without any necessary geographical link with the peninsula. On Sinai (in the broad sense) the Christian regards thinking as the generative force behind acting; he believes in the primacy of *logos* over *ethos*, of theory over practice. At Studion he wonders: how should I act? At Sinai the question is rather: how should I think?

Sinaite spirituality has a certain affective flavor that distinguishes it from Basilian and Studite sobriety. Its piety is permeated by tenderness. Something of this tenderness appears already in the sayings of the first Desert Fathers. The combination of Desert spirituality with tenderness will seem in no way surprising to those of us who have read, in our time, the writings of Fr Charles de Foucauld. This tenderness is concentrated upon the person, the remembrance and the name of Christ. By preference one invokes the name "Jesus" on its own, and that is already significant. The Jesus

35

Prayer was to be born and to flourish in this atmosphere.[1]
It was on Sinai, so we may recall, that God had long ago
revealed his name to Moses.

Of the various witnesses to this spirituality, the earliest
in date seems to be St Diadochus, Bishop of Photike
around 458.[2] In his *Hundred Chapters on Perfection* he

---

[1]Fr Irénée Hausherr has very rightly called attention to the affective side of
Sinaite spirituality and its role in relation to the Jesus Prayer in *La Méthode
d'oraison hésychaste (Orientalia Christiana* IX, 2, no. 36: Rome, 1927), p. 120. Since
then, however, he seems to have changed his mind. He now sees in the Sinaites
"merely transmitters," whose spirituality came from Egypt and Palestine and
constitutes "a subdivision of Hesychast spirituality" *(Noms du Christ et voies
d'oraison* [*Orientalia Christiana Analecta* 157: Rome, 1960], p. 248; English translation by Charles Cummings, *The Name of Jesus* [*Cistercian Studies Series* 44:
Kalamazoo, 1978], p. 279). Perhaps the question remains open. See also the
interesting article of E.J. Ryan, "The Invocation of the Name in Sinaite Spirituality,"
in *Eastern Churches Quarterly* 14 (1961-2), pp. 241-9, 291-9.

We would like to add this. Fr Hausherr, in his book *Noms du Christ*, has
indicated unambiguously his disagreement with several of the views expressed by
"A Monk of the Eastern Church." But, even if he and we do not see everything in
the same way, we are bound to express our respect for the highly important
pioneer work that he has devoted to the Jesus Prayer. Others before him spoke
about it. But it may certainly be claimed that his work of 1927 on the Hesychast
method of prayer constituted the point of departure, the spiritual "shock," without
which a number of Christians would never have found their way to the name of
Jesus. And with all our heart we make our own these lines by Fr Hausherr in
Noms du Christ, p. 283 (English translation, p. 328): "It matters little that these
affirmations contradict what is said by the anonymous writer in the *Philokalia* and
by 'A Monk of the Eastern Church.' What should be emphaized is that, in each
case, the representatives of these three opinions intend and desire to invoke the
name of the Savior. . .This agreement between all of them over what is
fundamental and over the final aim matters far more to us than any disagreement
over formulas or explanations. 'What of it? Whatever the way in which Christ is
invoked, I rejoice at it, and will always rejoice.' " (Cf. Phil 1:18)

It is impossible to read without emotion the passage in which Fr Hausherr tells
us how, such was the joy he experienced in gathering together the names of Jesus
from works of every type, that he immersed himself in this task so completely as
almost to lose the last vestiges of his eyesight; and also the passage in which he
rebuts the charge of not showing total sympathy for *every* human effort towards
pure and unceasing prayer. Those who, influenced by some words that he wrote
about Hesychasm long ago, have been led to misinterpret his sentiments, need feel
no further reservations when they come across his clear declaration: "Nothing that
concerns Christ leaves me indifferent. His names above all, because in a certain
sense these are identified with his Person."

[2]For the Greek text (with French translation) of the *Hundred Chapters on
Perfection*, see the edition of E. des Places *(Sources chrétiennes* 5 ter: Paris, 1966);
English translation in G.E.H. Palmer, P. Sherrard and K. Ware, *The Philokalia*, vol.
1 (London, 1979), pp. 252-96. Cf. F. Doerr, *Diadochus von Photike und die*

recommends purifying the heart through the "remembrance of Jesus,"[3] which, indeed, not only purifies but inflames. "We ought", he says, "to give to the intellect (*nous*) nothing but the words *Lord Jesus* (τὸ Κύριε Ἰησοῦ)."[4] Let us take note of this phrase. The Jesus Prayer exists from this point onwards as a formula and a technique. Diadochus is a spiritual teacher of great interest to whom full credit has still not been given.

Also representative of Sinaite spirituality are those two inseparable saints, Barsanuphius and John, who are slightly later in date than Diadochus. St Barsanuphius (†about 540), of Egyptian origin, lived in a monastery near Gaza. He was called the "great old man," ὁ μέγας γέρων, and, although he was not a priest, the faithful attributed to him the power of forgiving sins, even at a distance. There is a perfect identity of thought between Barsanuphius and his friend John the Prophet. From these two "elders" we have more than 840 spiritual letters, about 446 of them by John and 396 by Barsanuphius.[5] These letters are not a correspondence be-

---

Messalianer (Freiburg im Breisgau, 1937); H. Doerries, "Diadochus und Symeon. Das Verhältnis der κεφάλαια γνωστικά zum Messalianismus," in *Worte und Stünde*, vol. 1 (Göttingen, 1966), pp. 352-422; and the article by K. Popov on Diadochus and the Jesus Prayer (in Russian) in *Trudy Kievskoi dukhovnoi Akademii* 3 (1902), pp. 651-76. [See also Kallistos Ware, "The Jesus Prayer in St Diadochus of Photice," in G.D. Dragas (ed.), *Aksum - Thyateira: A Festschrift for Archbishop Methodios of Thyateira and Great Britain* (London, 1985), pp. 557-68.]

[About a generation prior to Diadochus, St Nilus of Ancyra (†about 430) refers several times in the course of his voluminous correspondence to the "remembrance" or "invocation" of the name of Jesus: see *Letters* II, 140 and 214; III, 273 and 278 (*PG* 79, cols. 260A, 261D, 312C, 520C, 521C). Cf. Hausherr, *Noms du Christ*, pp. 195-6; *The Name of Jesus*, p. 212.]

[3]§97.

[4]§59.

[5]The first edition of the Greek text, prepared by St Nicodemus of the Holy Mountain, only appeared after his death (Vienna, 1816); reissued by S.N. Schoinas (Volos, 1960). There is a critical edition of part of the Greek text, with English translation, by Derwas J. Chitty in *Patrologia Orientalis* XXXI, 3 (Paris, 1966), and a French translation of the whole collection by L. Regnault and P. Lemaire (Solesmes, 1972). Cf. I. Hausherr, in *Dictionnaire de Spiritualité* 1 (1937), cols. 1255-62; F. Neyt, "La prière de Jésus," in *Collectanea Cisterciensia* 34 (1972), pp. 202-17; English translation, "The Prayer of Jesus," in *Sobornost* 6, no. 9 (1974), pp. 641-54.

[There are also important references to the Jesus Prayer in *The Life of*

tween the two friends, but are addressed to outside persons.
The two writers recommend abandonment of one's own
will, spiritual direction, examination of conscience and,
finally, the invocation of the name of Jesus. John disap-
proved of the "antirrhetic" method or method of contradiction (we may recall the *Antirrhetikos* of Evagrius), which
consists in confronting temptations face to face in combat
or direct dispute. This method is right only for those who
are "powerful in God," for those who are "like St Michael."
There is another way. "For us, the weak, the only way is to
take refuge in the name of Jesus." Here is one of the most
beautiful statements in the whole of the literature about the
Jesus Prayer. Barsanuphius raises the question which is
preferable: the Jesus Prayer or psalmody. He replies: "One
must practice both." The Hesychasts of Athos were to be
more radical and demand that the Jesus Prayer absorb all
other prayer. The letters of Barsanuphius and John enjoyed
great success in Russia where, since the 18th century, they
have been translated many times.

St John Climacus (†around 649) was a Sinaite in the full
geographical sense of the word, since he became a monk
on the peninsula at the age of sixteen and was successively
a cenobite, an anchorite and a monastic superior at Sinai.[6]
His *Ladder of Paradise*[7] is the classic treatise of Sinaite

Dositheus by Dorotheus of Gaza, disciple of Barsanuphius and John: see the
edition by L. Regnault in *Sources chrétiennes* 92 (Paris, 1963), pp. 122-45, especially §10. Also significant for the early history of the Jesus Prayer is the *Discourse
on Abba Philemon* in the *Philokalia*: Greek text, edition of the publishing house
"Astir," vol. 2 (Athens, 1958), pp. 241-52; English translation in Palmer, Sherrard
and Ware, *The Philokalia*, vol. 2 (London, 1981), pp. 344-57. This work of
uncertain date (?6th-7th century), describing the life of an Egyptain monk,
contains—to our knowledge, for the first time in any surviving text—what may be
regarded as the "standard formula" of the Jesus Prayer, "Lord Jesus Christ, Son of
God, have mercy on me" (formulas closely similar to this occur in Barsanuphius
and John, and also in Dorotheus, but with minor variations). Cf. Hieromonk (later
Archbishop) Basile Krivochéine, "Date du texte traditionnel de la 'Prière de Jésus',"
in *Messager de l'Exarchat du Patriarche russe en Europe occidentale* 7-8 (1951),
pp. 55-59; Hausherr, *Noms du Christ*, pp. 239-45; *The Name of Jesus*, pp. 270-7.]
    [6]H. Delehaye, *Synaxarium Ecclesiae Constantinopolitanae* (Brussels, 1902), pp.
571-4; G. Couilleau, in *Dictionnaire de Spiritualité* 8 (1972), cols. 369-89.
    [7]*PG* 88, cols. 632-1208. There is a better edition of the Greek text by the monk
Sophronios (Constantinople, 1883); reprinted by the publishing house "Astir"

spirituality. The ideal prayer for him was one which eliminates discursive elements or *logismoi*, and becomes prayer of a single word or phrase, *monologia*. The "remembrance of Jesus" provides this prayer with its content and form. In his spiritual teaching is found an anticipation of future Hesychast theories which associate the Jesus Prayer with the perception of a supernatural light, for according to John the "eye of the heart" is able to see the divine "Sun of the intelligence" and, when this happens, the contemplative beholds himself as completely luminous. The principal text of the *Ladder* on the invocation of the name is this: "May the remembrance of Jesus be united to your breathing, and then you will know the value of *hesychia*."[8] There is no doubt that for the Sinaites the "remembrance of Jesus" was not just a simple mnemonic device, but was firmly founded upon the divine name. That is why John suggests that we should in some way "fasten" to our breathing the remembrance of the name of Jesus, thereby enabling our life of contemplation to come to true fulfillment. This idea was, as we shall see, destined to a strange fortune.

*

*   *

The *Centuries* attributed to Hesychius are one of the most important texts in the literature of the Jesus Prayer.[9] The work has been erroneously attributed to St Hesychius, a priest at Jerusalem (†about 450), who has, however, no connection with Hesychasm. The *Centuries* are the work of an author, or more probably of several authors, associated

---

(Athens, 1970). [An improved Greek text, with modern Greek translation, has been edited by Archimandrite Ignatios (Monastery of the Paraclete, Oropos, Attica, 1978). English translation of the *Ladder* by Colm Luibheid and Norman Russell (*The Classics of Western Spirituality*: New York, 1982); on Climacus' teaching about the Jesus Prayer, see the introduction by Kallistos Ware, pp. 45-53.]

[8]*Ladder* 27 (*PG* 88, col. 1112C).

[9]*PG* 93, cols. 1480-1544; English translation in Palmer, Sherrard and Ware, *The Philokalia*, vol.1, pp. 162-98. Cf. J. Kirchmeyer, in *Dictionnaire de Spiritualité* 7 (1971), cols. 408-10.

with the monastery of Batos (the burning bush) on Sinai. The work is later than St John Climacus, since it quotes him. And the passage quoted is precisely this: "May the remembrance of Jesus be united to your breathing. . ." Hesychius continues: ". . .and to your whole life."[10] The addition is important. It is not simply prayer, it is our whole life that is to be controlled by the "remembrance of Jesus." The spirituality of the name grows ever more and more all-embracing. The *Centuries* speak of the prayer as "monologic," *monologistos*. The work uses the term "Jesus Prayer" (εὐχὴ τοῦ Ἰησοῦ), and this is to our knowledge the earliest appearance of this phrase, although the reality that it denotes was already well known. The work also employs the expression ἐπίκλησις Ἰησοῦ, "call," "invocation," "epiclesis" of Jesus. Sometimes it speaks of the "holy name of Christ."

The Jesus Prayer must be "breathed" continually.[11] When the intellect has been purified and unified by it, our thoughts swim in it as merry dolphins in a peaceful sea.[12] Then a dialogue begins in which Christ, who has become the inner master, makes known his will to the heart.[13] When the Jesus Prayer is understood in this way, clearly its final aim is not mystical silence but the hearing of the divine word. We do not remain exterior to the name invoked, but the invocation allows us to "participate in the holy name of Jesus."[14] It gives us the virtues of temperance and continence. The name of Jesus comes into our life first of all as a lamp in the darkness; next it is like moonlight, and finally like the sunrise.[15] Being the sun of our intellect, it creates within it luminous thoughts, to which it communicates its own splendor, thoughts resembling the sun.[16] It is

---

[10]*Cent.* I, 99. [The words "and to your whole life" are absent from the Greek text as given in the *Philokalia*.]

[11]*Cent.* II, 85, 87.

[12]*Cent.* II, 54.

[13]*Cent.* II, 84.

[14]*Cent.* I, 96.

[15]*Cent.* II, 64.

[16]*Cent.* II, 94.

love which elevates us—we should notice the part played by divine love in this process of transformation—and makes us πρωτάγγελοι, higher than angels.[17] To pronounce the name of Jesus in a holy way is an all-sufficient and surpassing aim for any human life. "Truly blessed," proclaim the *Centuries*, "is he who unceasingly pronounces in his heart the name of Jesus, and who in the depths of his mind is united to the Jesus Prayer as the body to the surrounding air and as wax to the flame."[18]

The *Capita alia* which appear in Migne under the name of St Maximus the Confessor (†662)) insist on "monologic" prayer.[19] Are these fragments actually by Maximus? Arguments can be advanced both for and against. It is possible that Maximus is indeed the author of these texts, and very probable that he was acquainted with John Climacus' teaching on the Jesus Prayer.

*

*   *

In the 8th and 9th centuries no outstanding texts concerning the Jesus Prayer are known. The Prayer existed; it was recommended; it already formed part of the Byzantine spiritual tradition. But it remains, as it were, somewhat

---

[17]*Cent.* II, 69.

[18]*Cent.* II, 94. [Closely linked with Hesychius is another Sinaite writer, Philotheus, author of a short work entitled *Forty Texts on Watchfulness:* Greek text in the "Astir" edition of the *Philokalia*, vol. 2 (Athens, 1958), pp. 274-86; English translation in Palmer, Sherrard and Ware, *The Philokalia*, vol. 3 (London, 1984), pp. 16-31. His date is hard to determine; probably later than Climacus, he may have lived in the 8th-9th century, or even later. The Jesus Prayer, he says, has power to "concentrate the scattered intellect *(nous)*" (27); and, anticipating the 14th-century Hesychasts, he speaks of a "luminous reflection" of Jesus Christ within the soul (23).]

[19]*PG* 90, cols. 1401-61; English translation in Palmer, Sherrard and Ware, *The Philokalia*, vol. 3 (London, 1984), pp. 34-65. [The ascription to Maximus is certainly erroneous. The work appears in *PG* 127, cols. 1129-76, and in the *Philokalia*, attributed to its true author, Elias Ecdicus (?11th-12th century). It seems unlikely that Maximus had read John Climacus.]

fluid. There is still no trace of the psycho-physiological techniques which were to appear later. The very form of the Prayer does not seem to be fixed. The name of Jesus is obviously a necessary element within it, its center and its source of power. Yet great freedom is allowed in its use. It appears that some pronounced the name alone, while others associated it with some short invocation. In order to find the Jesus Prayer in some measure crystallized, we must wait for the appearance of a work of uncertain date and authorship, but of decisive importance and influence, the *Method of Holy Prayer and Attention* (Μέθοδος τῆς ἱερᾶς προσευχῆς καὶ προσοχῆς). Migne gives this work only in a neo-Greek version.[20] To Fr Irénée Hausherr, SJ, we are indebted for the first critical edition of the *Method* based on the principal manuscripts.[21]

A general and uninterrupted tradition has attributed the *Method* to St Symeon the New Theologian (949-1022),[22] abbot of the monastery of St Mamas in Constantinople. Already in the 17th century Combefis and in our day Holl, Papamikhail, Stein and Stavrou have called this attribution in question. Fr Hausherr rejects it categorically; he even believes that he has established the identity of the true author, who is in his view a monk of Mount Athos, Nicephoros, of whom we shall speak again later.[23] Fr Hausherr's arguments have not convinced the Byzantine scholar, Fr Martin Jugie, AA.[24] After studying the arguments, the

---

[20]*PG* 120, cols. 701-710.

[21]I. Hausherr, *La Méthode d'oraison hésychaste (Orientalia Christiana* IX, 2, no. 36: Rome, 1927), pp. 150-72; English translation (from the Russian) in E. Kadloubovsky and G.E.H. Palmer, *Writings from the Philokalia on Prayer of the Heart* (London, 1951), pp. 152-61.

[22]With Symeon we enter into a period in which the Roman and Byzantine lists of saints no longer coincide. Symeon himself almost found a place, through an oversight, in the *Acta Sanctorum*, but the Dominican Combefis (†1679) dissuaded the Bollandists from allowing him to appear in it. In our use of the epithet "St" we conform to a purely historical criterion, giving this title to the various persons who have obtained it in their own Church.

[23]I. Hausherr, *La Méthode d'oraison hésychaste;* also "Note sur l'inventeur de la Méthode d'oraison hésychaste," in *Orientalia Christiana* XX, no. 66 (1930), pp. 179-82, reprinted in *Hésychasme et prière,* pp. 4-7.

[24]M. Jugie, "Les origines de la méthode d'oraison des hésychastes," in *Echos*

reader will probably incline towards the solution proposed by Fr Hausherr. Nevertheless it seems to us better to leave this question open. Therefore we shall speak about the *Method* without prejudging the problem of its origin. But the *Method* is so dependent on the spiritual atmosphere created by Symeon, even though he is not its author, that a few lines about the abbot of St Mamas will help us to understand this atmosphere.

St Symeon the New Theologian has been compared by his admirers to the author of the Fourth Gospel.[25] His is certainly the greatest name in the history of post-patristic Byzantine spirituality. If it is true that the Orthodox and the Roman Church have been separated from each other more by certain spiritual tendencies than by conflicts on the strictly dogmatic and historical levels, then it must be said that Symeon, and two centuries later St Gregory Palamas, have had a greater share than Photius and Cerularius in the divergence of the "two mentalities." Through his views on the ministry of the "spiritual father" and on the necessity of

---

d'Orient 30 (1931), pp. 179-85; cf. *Echos d'Orient* 35 (1936), pp. 409-12. [It should be noted that one of Jugie's main arguments against the ascription of the work to Nicephoros is not valid. He appeals to *Vatic. gr.* 658, one of the manuscripts containing the work, which he dates to the 11th-12th century; but this probably belongs to the 14th century.]

[25] [Most of Symeon's writings are now available, with a French translation, in the series *Sources chrétiennes: Catecheses* (vols. 96, 104, 113); *Theological and Ethical Discourses* (vols. 122, 129); *Theological, Gnostic and Practical Chapters* (vol. 51 bis); *Hymns* (vols, 156, 174, 196). For the *Letter on Confession*, see K. Holl, *Enthusiasmus und Bussgewalt beim Griechischen Mönchtum. Eine Studie zu Symeon dem Neuen Theologen* (Leipzig, 1898), pp. 110-27; an edition of this and the other letters of Symeon is awaited in *Sources chrétiennes*. There is an English translation of the *Catecheses* (or *Discourses*) by C.J. de Catanzaro (*The Classics of Western Spirituality*: New York, 1980); of the *Theological Discourses* and the *Chapters* by P. McGuckin (*Cistercian Studies Series* 44: Kalamazoo, 1982); of the *Hymns* by G.A. Maloney (Denville, NJ, no date: ?1975). The *Life* of Symeon by Nicetas Stethatos has been edited with a French translation by I. Hausherr and G. Horn, in *Orientalia Christiana* XII, no. 45 (Rome, 1928). See also G.A. Maloney, *The Mystic Fire and Light: St. Symeon the New Theologian* (Denville, NJ, 1975); Archbishop Basile Krivochéine, *In the Light of Christ. St. Symeon the New Theologian: Life, Spirituality, Doctrine*, translated by Anthony Gythiel (Crestwood, NY, 1987), originally published as *Dans la lumière du Christ: Saint Syméon le Nouveau Théologien* (Chevetogne, 1980); B. Fraigneau-Julien, *Les sens spirituels et la vision de Dieu selon Syméon le Nouveau Théologien* (Paris, 1985).

mystical experience, Symeon, possibly without intending to
do so, has contributed to a certain conception of the "primacy of the spiritual," understood as the primacy of the
pneumatic and charismatic element over the hierarchical
and institutional, and also as the primacy of contemplation
over intellectual and active life. These notions or rather
these attitudes are still more or less latent in the Orthodox
soul. They have been developed by certain Russian schools
of theology which show a special partiality for them; and
they have marked Orthodoxy with an imprint as strong as
that with which the Counter-Reformation, the Council of
Trent and the First Vatican Council have marked the
Roman Church.

But what interests us here is Symeon's relationship to the
Jesus Prayer. Putting aside the treatise on the *Method*, we
find in Symeon's writings no direct reference to this prayer.
However, three comments are necessary.

First of all, the Jesus Prayer as it is described in the
Method would not have been unanimously and continually
attributed to Symeon if the Hesychast monastic circles,
where Symeon's memory was especially alive, had not
noticed a close connection between this Prayer and the
spirituality of the abbot of St Mamas. We are strongly
inclined to believe that the details of the Method are not
due to Symeon; but it is more than likely that Symeon drew
upon John Climacus and Hesychius, that he himself advocated this prayer which in his time was already regarded
as the contemplative prayer *par excellence,* and that he
inspired his disciples to make further developments in the
practice of this prayer. It should be noted that Symeon,
while himself following the Studite life, was permeated
with the Sinaite spirituality in which the name of Jesus
occupied a privileged place. Indeed, this Sinaite influence
was one of the reasons for the difficulties encountered by
Symeon in his relationship with the Studite *milieu.*

In the second place, Symeon's extraordinary Christocentrism predisposed him towards the Jesus Prayer. In the
whole of the Byzantine Middle Ages there was no writer

more Christocentric than Symeon. Any history of the love shown to Christ would need to assign a special place to him. Symeon expressed his love for Jesus with the most moving tenderness, with the most vivid lyrical feeling. His theology is essentially a theology of the "body of Christ." We do not say "mystical body of Christ," because this is an expression foreign to Patristic tradition; but Symeon was indeed concerned with man's incorporation in Christ. It is well known that the Greek tradition envisaged this incorporation in a more realistic way than the Latin West has done. Beyond a mere analogy between the local structure of the Church and the human biological organism, beyond even an incorporation by grace, the Greek Fathers, without falling into any kind of pantheistic identification, based their conception of the body of Christ on the idea that the Logos has assumed human nature; and this last, in their way of thinking, is very similar to the Platonic Form or Idea of humanity. Symeon develops the theme of our incorporation in Christ with such physiological realism that his Latin editors were scandalized by it. When the reader of Migne reached the most daring passages in the *Hymns of Divine Love,* he was confronted by a cut and a note in which the Jesuit Father Pontanus (Jacob Spanmuller, †1626) declared that this kind of development was "best passed over in silence, being hardly worthy of Latin ears" *(silentio praetermittendam, latinisque auribus non satis dignam);* the Jesuit Father spoke also of "ideas that are scarcely pious or decent" *(nec satis aut piae aut decentes. . .considerationes).*[26] Now is there any prayer more Christocentric than the Jesus Prayer? Is there any prayer that expresses better our incorporation in Christ? is there any prayer in which Jesus becomes to such a degree the very substance of our speech and thought? That is why, in a history of the Jesus Prayer, Symeon is *absens quidem nomine, praesens autem spiritu,* "absent indeed by name, but present in spirit."

---

[26]*PG* 120, col. 531, note 19. [For the original Greek text (without omissions!), see *Hymn* XV, especially lines 141-67 *(Sources chrétiennes* 156, pp. 288-91); English translation by Maloney, pp. 54-55.]

Nor is this all. It seems that we possess definite evidence on the link uniting Symeon to the Jesus Prayer. Symeon's biographer, Nicetas Stethatos, reports the following episode during his hero's youth: ". . .At that time he was filled during prayer with great joy and suffused with burning tears. Not yet initiated into such revelations, in his amazement he cried aloud continually, 'Lord, have mercy'. . .In this light, then, he received the strength to see; and so it was that, toward the heights of heaven, there appeared to him a kind of highly luminous cloud, without form or shape, full of the ineffable glory of God. . .Finally, much later, when this light gradually withdrew, he found himself again in his body and inside his cell, and he felt his heart filled with an indescribable joy, while his mouth cried aloud, as has been said, 'Lord have mercy,' and his whole person was suffused with tears sweeter than honey."[27] We find in this account the joy of heart and the vision of light that Hesychasm was later to associate with the Jesus Prayer.

But was Symeon's "Lord, have mercy. . ." addressed to Christ? One of Symeon's writings would prompt us to reply in the affirmative. Symeon is the author of a discourse on the necessity of mystical experience.[28] In this discourse he describes an experience identical to that reported by Nicetas, without stating however that he himself was the subject of the experience. The man, says Symeon, who undergoes this experience of light, of sweetness and tears, knows that "someone is appearing before his face." Then a dialogue begins: "My God, is it you?" "Yes, it is I, God, who became man for you." Thus it is the person of Jesus who appears to Symeon. Now if, as we suspect, Symeon is relating here the ecstatic vision that he had in his youth, his prayer, "Lord, have mercy," must be addressed to Christ. This is not yet the Jesus Prayer, in the sense that

---

[27][*Life* 5. Compare Symeon's own account of the vision in *Catechesis* 22, lines 88-112; here, however, he prays, not with the words *Kyrie eleison*, but with the prayer of the Publican in Lk 18:13, "God be merciful to me a sinner."]

[28]The text and translation are given by Hausherr in *La Méthode d'oraison hésychaste*, pp. 174-207; the same piece appears as *Ethical Discourse* 5 in *Sources chrétiennes*, vol. 129, pp. 78-119.

the actual name of Jesus is missing from it. But the union of "Lord, have mercy" with the thought of Jesus already points forward to a formula in which the phrase "Lord, have mercy" and the actual name of Jesus will be united; and it is just such a formula that probably, if not certainly, the treatise on the *Method* presents to us.

This treatise, which we must now analyze, begins with a warning against the dangers of using the imagination in prayer. As well as prayer of the imagination, there is (we are told) an alternative form of prayer that consists in struggling violently against evil thoughts; but this method has many difficulties. There is also a third form of prayer. Before considering it, we should note that it presupposes obedience, without which there is no pure conscience. It presupposes also "keeping guard over the heart," which permits one without difficulty to attain everything else.

This brings us to the central passage in the work. In order to pray, it is said, the disciple must close the door of his cell, place himself in a state of quiet, sit down, rest his chin against his chest, look towards the middle of his stomach, restrain his breathing, and make a mental effort to find the "place of the heart," while repeating all the time "the epiclesis of Jesus Christ."[29] At the beginning he experiences only difficulty and obscurity, but soon he notices a kind of light. From this point onwards, as soon as an evil thought arises, and even before it comes to completion and takes form, it is expelled and destroyed. "Through the invocation of the Lord Jesus, the winds of the passions dissolve and vanish like wax." However, this result is not obtained in a single day. One must go through the successive stages of domination over the passions, of the sweet-

---

[29][Although the directions given are not altogether clear, it seems that the author of the *Method* regards the control of breathing as a preliminary exercise that precedes rather than accompanies the "epiclesis of Jesus Christ." The "epiclesis" or "invocation" commences only after the disciple, through the use of the psychosomatic technique, had already found the "place of the heart." In the treatise *Guarding the Heart* by Nicephoros, the breathing technique is likewise regarded as a preliminary exercise before commencing the Jesus Prayer. In Gregory of Sinai and in Kallistos and Ignatius Xanthopoulos, however, the control of the breathing accompanies the actual recitation of the Prayer.]

ness of psalmody, and then of the substitution of the Jesus
Prayer for psalmody; so finally one attains *theoria*, contemplation that is firmly established and undeviating. In this
way the spiritual house is built into which Christ will come.
All this is not beyond our reach. "The rest you will learn
with the help of God by keeping watch over your intellect
and by holding Jesus in your heart; as the saying goes, sit
in your cell, and your cell will teach you all things." A
delightful phrase that could have been written by the
author of the *Imitation*.

We notice that the *Method* does not give any definite
formula for the Jesus Prayer; it speaks only of the invocation or "epiclesis" of Jesus. So it is in the Greek manuscripts and in the critical text based on the manuscripts by
Fr Hausherr. But the neo-Greek version of the *Method*,
which is found in Migne and which is sometimes a para-
phrase, twice gives the formula: "Lord Jesus Christ, have
mercy on me." The neo-Greek version is not anterior to the
18th century; but it bears witness to what is surely a very
ancient traditional interpretation of the "epiclesis of Jesus."
It is more than possible, it is likely, that the formula "Lord
Jesus Christ, have mercy on me" is what the *Method* in-
tends when it speaks of the invocation of the name. In any
case, this is an interpretation that was already current in the
13th and 14th centuries.

*

*   *

A reading of the *Method* leaves on us a rather complex
impression. On the one hand, it offers classic advice about
the spiritual life. On the other, there is the innovation, at
first sight frankly disconcerting, whereby the invocation of
the name is linked to certain psycho-physiological methods.
We shall come back to this point later. Fr Hausherr's thesis,
attributing the *Method* to the Athonite monk Nicephoros,

seems probable enough if .we compare the *Method* with the treatise on *Guarding the Heart,* of which Nicephoros is indeed the author.[30]

Nicephoros advocates the Jesus Prayer, accompanied by a holding back within the heart of the air that is breathed in, so as to facilitate, as he puts it, the entrance of the intellect (*nous*) into the heart. The most important statement of Nicephoros' treatise is this: "Take away all discursive thought from the reason (you can if you so desire) and give to it the invocation, 'Lord Jesus Christ, Son of God, have mercy on me'; and force yourself, in place of all other thoughts, always to cry out this prayer within yourself."[31] The actual formula of the prayer has here been expanded by the addition "Son of God." At the same time, as the very title of the treatise indicates, Nicephoros presents the Jesus Prayer in an ascetical context borrowed from the Fathers and closely consistent with traditional spirituality. It is difficult to date this treatise. According to Athonite tradition, Nicephoros was a monk on the Holy Mountain about 1340, enjoying a great reputation for sanctity there; he was one of Gregory Palamas' masters. Strangely enough, Nicephoros was of Latin origin.[32] But all this is doubtful. Perhaps he should rather be dated to the 12th or 13th century.

Beyond doubt the letter addressed to monks, preserved among the writings of Chrysostom, must have been written

---

[30]*PG* 147, cols. 945-66; English translation (from the Russian) in Kadloubovsky and Palmer, *Writings from the Philokalia on the Prayer of the Heart,* pp. 22-34.

[31]*Ibid.,* cols. 965-6.

[32]Nicodemus of the Holy Mountain, Ἀκολουθία τῶν ὁσίων πατέρων τοῦ ῞Αθω (Hermoupolis, 1847), p. 115. [More precise information on Nicephoros is supplied in Gregory Palamas, *Triads in Defense of the Holy Hesychasts* I, 2, 12: II, 2, 2 (ed. J. Meyendorff, *Spicilegium Sacrum Lovaniense* 31-32, vol. i, pp. 99, 321-3). Palamas dates Nicephoros to the last part of the 13th century, stating that he was one of those who was persecuted for resisting the Unionist policies of Michael VIII Palaeologus (reigned 1259-82) after the Council of Lyons (1274); and he confirms that Nicephoros was by origin an Italian (i.e. probably a Greek from Calabria in South Italy). It is just possible, although unlikely, that Nicephoros was still alive when Palamas arrived on Athos around 1317; more probably he was Palamas' "master" only in the broader sense that Palamas was influenced by him and defended his memory. In any event, he cannot have survived as late as 1340.]

after Nicephoros' time.[33] Its editor, in Migne, calls it *omnino futilis et inepta*. This appraisal seems to us altogether unjust. The unknown author tells us in substance that we are to overcome all evil thoughts by invoking the name of Jesus. We are to repeat from morning to night, "Lord Jesus Christ, Son of God, have mercy on us." We should pray in this way while eating and drinking. We are to call to mind Jesus Christ until the name of the Lord penetrates our heart, descends to its very depths, crushes the dragon and gives life to the soul. Our heart is to absorb the Lord and the Lord to absorb our heart, and the two are to become one. This is not the task of one or two days, but requires time and exertion. It is something that we can do everywhere; it is not restricted to the church building: "You are a temple; do not look for a place." We may note that the author uses Nicephoros' formula, but replaces the singular pronoun with the plural "us." We notice also that he makes no mention of a physical technique.

About the year 1200, the nun Theodora, daughter of the Emperor Isaac Angelos, exchanged letters with a certain Abba Isaias who has generally been confused with a Monophysite writer of the 5th century. This Abba Isaias earnestly recommends Theodora to use the *Kyrie Eleison*. One may wonder whether, for Isaias, *Kyrie Eleison* retained the general significance of an invocation to God, such as it had among the Desert Fathers, or if *Kyrios*, as frequently happens in the New Testament, here designates specifically the person of Christ. What makes the second alternative probable is the fact that Isaias incorporates in his letters a passage preserved in the Athonite manuscript *Codex Panteleimon 571*, a text already used by Nicephoros who clearly connects it with the Jesus Prayer.[34] In that case Isaias' letters

---

[33]*PG* 60, cols. 752-5. Cf. Hausherr, *Noms du Christ*, pp. 200-202; *The Name of Jesus*, pp. 217-20.

[34]I. Hausherr, "Note sur l'inventeur de la méthode d'oraison hésychaste," in *Orientalia Christiana* XX, no. 66 (1930), p. 180, n. l; *Hésychasme et prière*, p. 5, n. l. Cf. I. Hausherr, "Le Métérikon de l'abbé Isaie," in *Orientalia Christiana Periodica* 12 (1946), pp. 286-301; reprinted in *Etudes de spiritualité orientale (Orientalia Christiana Analecta* 183: Rome, 1969), pp. 105-20.

enable us to trace, at close quarters, the process whereby the use of *Kyrie eleison* leads eventually to the Jesus Prayer.

CHAPTER III

THE JESUS PRAYER
IN ATHONITE HESYCHASM

St Gregory the Sinaite (†1346) represents, in the history
of the Jesus Prayer, the end of the Sinaite phase and the
beginning of the Athonite phase. He himself, while in
Crete, received from the monk Arsenius the tradition of the
Jesus Prayer; he went next to Athos and then retired to
Mount Katakryomenos.[1] He certainly did not introduce the
Jesus Prayer at Athos; indeed Athos, as regards the Prayer,
did not differ essentially from Sinai. What Gregory did was
to revive the flame. When he came to Athos, he found only
three monks there, Isaias, Cornelius and Macarius, who
were experienced in contemplative life. But, from Gregory's
time onwards, it was Athos and no longer Sinai which
constituted the main center for the practice and diffusion of
the Jesus Prayer. On Athos the Prayer lost its original
fluidity. By degrees Athos restricted the Prayer to a fixed
formula in which no variations were permitted—*ne varietur*
—and it insisted in particular on the accompanying psycho-

---

[1][For the Greek text of Gregory's work, see *PG* 150, cols. 1240-1345; English
translation (from the Russian) in Kadloubovsky and Palmer, *Writings from the
Philokalia on Prayer of the Heart*, pp. 37-94. Cf. J. Bois, "Grégoire le Sinaïte et
l'hésychasme à l'Athos au XIVe siècle," in *Echos d'Orient* 5 (1901), pp. 65-73; V.
Kiselkov, *Gregory the Sinaite as a representative of mysticism at Byzantium in the
Fourteenth Century* (in Bulgarian) (Sofia, 1938); J. Darrouzès, in *Dictionnaire de
Spiritualité* 6 (1967), cols. 1011-14; Kallistos Ware, "The Jesus Prayer in St Gregory
of Sinai," in *Eastern Churches Review* 4 (1972), pp. 3-22; H.V. Beyer, "Die
Lichtlehre der Mönche des Vierzehnten und des Vierten Jahrhunderts, erörtert am
Beispiel des Gregorios Sinaïtes, des Euagrios Pontikos und des Ps. Makarios/Symeon,"
in XVI *Internationaler Byzantinisten-Kongress*, Akten 1/2 *(Jahrbuch der Osterrei-
chischen Byzantinistik* 31/2: Vienna, 1981), pp. 473-512; David Balfour, *Saint
Gregory the Sinaïte: Discourse on the Transfiguration* (reprint from *Theologia*:
Athens, 1983).]

physiological technique. In short, Athos exhibited greater
rigidity. Something of the tenderness and spontaneity of
Sinai was lost on the Holy Mountain, and this we may
regret.

All this, however, does not apply to Gregory of Sinai
himself. Three of his works are of special interest to the
history of spirituality. In his treatise *On Stillness and Prayer*,[2]
he sets out the theological foundations of the mystical life
in terms that the contemporary reader will find familiar
and attractive.[3] According to Gregory, the mystical life is
energeia, the active manifestation and operation of the
Spirit received at baptism; it is the discovery of a latent
gift, the rendering actual of what was potential. Gregory
distinguishes two ways whereby this may be achieved: the
way of the commandments, which requires much time and
work, and the way of the continual invocation or "epiclesis"
of the Lord Jesus. It is of course clearly understood that no
one can be dispensed from observing the commandments,
but the Jesus Prayer creates in us the humility and con-
trition that makes this *praxis* much easier.

His treatise *On Stillness and the Two Methods of
Prayer*[4] goes into concrete details. The spiritual aspirant
should devote himself to the Jesus Prayer in the morning.
He will remain seated, with his head lowered. He will
pronounce persistently the formula "Lord Jesus Christ, Son
of God, have mercy on me", bringing both his soul and his
intellect *(nous)* into play, immersing his intellect in his
heart. Pronouncing the name of Jesus, he will be nourished
by this divine name as by food (following out this line of
thought, we might explore the eucharistic use of the name
of Jesus, with the Jesus Prayer understood as a form of
spiritual communion). He will apply himself to giving full
meaning to each one of the words. Gregory allows a cer-

---

[2]*PG* 150, cols. 1304-12.
[3]Compare, for example, the work of Dom Anselm Stolz, *Théologie de la
mystique* (Chevetogne, 1939), English translation by Aidan Williams, *The Doctrine
of Spiritual Perfection* (St. Louis/London, 1938), which is in general very sympathetic to the Greek approach.
[4]*PG* 150, cols. 1313-29.

tain variety in the use of formulas: it is legitimate to alter-
nate between "Lord Jesus Christ, have mercy on me" and
"Son of God, have mercy on me", although one should not
change the formula of invocation too frequently, since
plants that are often transplanted do not take root. The
Jesus Prayer allows us to reach the state described by St
Paul: "It is no longer I that live, but Christ that lives in me"
(cf. Gal 2:20). A place is also to be allowed for psalmody
and reading.

The treatise *How a Hesychast should sit for Prayer and
Not Rise Up too soon*[5] returns to the question of the form
of words. Which formula is it better to use? Some say:
"Jesus, Son of God, have mercy on on me." To say in this
way "Jesus" instead of "Lord Jesus" is easier "because of
the weakness of our intellect." In point of fact, we know
from Scripture that no one can say that Jesus is the Lord
without a special inspiration from the Holy Spirit. One can
say "in a pure and perfect way" the words "Lord Jesus"
only in the Spirit (cf 1 Cor 12:3). It is better to refrain
from using these words than to repeat them thoughtlessly
like a child prattling away. On this last point we may
agree with Gregory or perhaps disagree; what remains
beyond dispute is the high spiritual vision expressed in his
writings.

*

*   *

At Mount Athos Gregory knew and greatly admired an
anchorite of the 14th century, St Maximus of Kapsokalyvia.[6]

---

[5] *PG* 150, cols. 1329-45.

[6] We possess no less than four biographies of Maximus, all of them written at
Athos, two in the 14th century by St Niphon and by Theophanes of Vatopedi, two
in the 15th century by Ioannicius Kochylas and by the monk-priest Macarius. The
biographies by Niphon and Theophanes were transcribed by a former monk of
Athos, Evlogios Kourilas, Bishop of Koritza, and edited by Fr Halkin in *Analecta
Bollandiana* 54 (1936), pp. 38-112. Bishop Evlogios also embarked on a work of
which only the first installment actually appreared: *History of Asceticism: the
Athonites*, vol. 1 (in Greek) (Thessalonica, 1929); this is almost entirely devoted to

Maximus was so enamored of the solitary life that many times he burned his hut (καλύβη, whence his surname "Kapsokalyvites," "of the burnt hut"), in order to escape the flow of visitors. He was credited with possessing the gift of discerning men's hearts. The Emperors John VI Cantacuzene and John V Palaeologus gladly consulted him. He told Gregory how with tears he had asked the Virgin Mary for the grace of "spiritual prayer" (the term is synonymous with the Jesus Prayer). As he stood before the icon of the Holy Virgin, he experienced a feeling of warmth and sweetness in his breast, and his heart began to say the Prayer. Maximus used to unite together "the remembrance of Jesus and the Mother of God" (μνήμη τοῦ Ἰησοῦ καὶ τῆς Θεοτόκου). We have seen that the expression "remembrance of Jesus" is equivalent to the invocation of the Name. Did Maximus use a formula in which the two names of Jesus and Mary were joined together? We cannot tell. But here we are confronted with a remarkable case—unique, so far as we are aware—in which the Jesus Prayer and prayer to the Virgin or the saints are in some way united. We shall see later, it is true, something analogus in the use of the Greek monastic rosary; but in the 14th century there seems to be no parallel instance. It shows how the Jesus Prayer and devotion to the Blessed Virgin Mary and the saints can be harmonized. Moreover, it indicates how Mary can form the Jesus Prayer within us. Maximus insists on the unification of our spirit through the Jesus Prayer; the spirit or intellect, he says, "become *monos* in the remembrance of Christ." Freeing ourselves of everything alien, we are to hold fast only to this remembrance and this prayer.

Theoleptus, Archbishop of Philadelphia, who died between 1310 and 1320, occupies in the history of the Jesus Prayer the place of a theoretical exponent—an exponent, that is, not of the psycho-physiological technique of the

---

the Skete τῶν καυσοκαλυβίων which, although founded in the 17th century, regards St Maximus of Kapsokalyvia as its first Father. Chapters 13, 14 and 15 of the biography of Maximus by Theophanes relate a discussion on prayer between Gregory the Sinaite and Maximus, and chapter 33 summarizes Maximus' teaching on this subject.

Prayer (bodily attitude, breathing, etc.), but of its psychology, of the mental operations which it implies.[7] Theoleptus is one of the spiritual authors who deserves to be rescued from unmerited oblivion. His works are for the most part

---

[7]See S. Salaville, "Formes ou méthodes de prière d'après un Byzantin du XIVe siècle, Théolepte de Philadelphie," in *Echos d'Orient* 39 (1940), pp. 1-25.

Fr Vitalien Laurent, in *Revue des Etudes byzantines* 17 (1959), p. 307, has been kind enough to make some comments on this present work, and for these we are grateful, although not agreeing with all of them. He feels that greater emphasis should have been placed on the distinction, evident in the Byzantine tradition, between the Jesus Prayer and prayer of the heart. Now it is quite true that in the early Byzantine period the two terms are not synonymous. But in current Orthodox usage, alike in monasticism and in the ordinary practice of the faithful, they have become virtually equivalent.

In regard to Theoleptus, Fr Laurent writes: "Could the author justify the title of saint ascribed to Theoleptus, archbishop (!) of Philadelphia?" In the original edition of this book we wrote "St Theoleptus"; on this point, however, Fr Laurent is undoubtedly right and we are wrong. Although there may have been a certain local cult, Theoleptus does not appear among the saints listed in the official calendar of the Greek Church. As for the exclamation mark that Fr Laurent places after the title archbishop, here we were following his learned colleague Fr Salaville, who in the article already cited (p. 2, n. l) calls Theoleptus "Metropolitan of Philadelphia." The precise date at which the Church of Philadelphia became a metropolis is hard to establish, but this seems to have occurred under Andronicus II Palaeologus (1283-1328), who was a contemporary of Theoleptus.

Fr Laurent adds that Theoleptus died, not between 1310 and 1320, but between 1324 and 1327. Here again, if we are in error, it is because we have followed Fr Salaville (see the article cited, p. 1). The dating of Theoleptus, and likewise of Nicephoros (to whom Fr Laurent also refers), seems to us so confused and uncertain that we cannot venture to propose a precise chronology. But what appears beyond question is that, as an inscription proves, Theoleptus was in charge of the Church of Philadelphia in 1305, and that he died before 16 January 1327, the date of the death of the author of his panegyric. Beyond this all seems conjectural and subject to caution.

Paula majora canamus. . .Fr Laurent does not share the very favorable opinion that we have expressed on the work of Theoleptus. "As for his work," he says, "which I am one of the few people to have read in its entirety, it is worthless." We continue, for our part, to value at a relatively high level this master of prayer. And here, once more, we find ourselves in agreement with Fr Séverien Salaville, who writes (art. cit., p. 25): "I sincerely believe that Theoleptus would have delighted Henri Bremond. . .Bremond would have viewed with satisfaction the harmonious and balanced combination in Theoleptus between ascetic effort and prayer, the first being no more than a means, a necessary means but a means none the less, to attain the second, which is the end. . .Theoleptus would have constituted for Bremond, in a modest but authentic manner, a forerunner of the mystics whom he venerated the most. . .Without making of Theoleptus a star of the first magnitude, Bremond would joyfully have recognized in him an interesting witness to Byzantine spirituality. . ."

unpublished.[8] He assigns to each one of our mental functions its respective role in the practice of the Jesus Prayer.
Our *dianoia*, our discursive intelligence or understanding,
conceives and repeats incessantly the name of the Lord.
Our *nous*, our intellectual or rational power, applies itself
entirely to this name. When invoking the name in our
"epiclesis," we make use of the faculty of speech, of the
word or *logos*. And finally the spirit, the *pneuma*, creates
in us compunction and love.

Theoleptus makes no mention of a definite formula of
invocation; he does not even say explicitly that the name
invoked is that of Jesus. But the terms "remembrance of
God," "name of the Lord," and "epiclesis" already possess
in the technical spiritual language of the 14th century a
meaning so precise that we have no hesitation in treating
them as synonymous with the Jesus Prayer. Moreover, Orthodox monastic tradition has long regarded Theoleptus as
one of the masters of this Prayer.

Theoleptus speaks of *logos* and *pneuma*. These words,
however, not only have a psychological meaning, but lead
us to the threshold of the mystery of the Trinity, since they
designate theologically the Word of God and the Holy
Spirit. In the tract reproduced in Migne, Theoleptus writes:
"Pure prayer reunites in itself the *nous*, the *logos* and the
pneuma. Through the *logos* it invokes God's name. Through
the *nous* it calmly fixes its gaze on the God whom it
invokes. Through the *pneuma* it manifests compunction,
humility and love. In this way it calls upon the eternal
Trinity, Father, Son and Holy Spirit, the one and only
God."[9]

According to Philotheus Kokkinos, Theoleptus was the
revered master of St Gregory Palamas (?1296-1359). The

---

[8]They can be found in the *Cod. Vatic. Ottob. graec.* 405: Περὶ νήψεως καὶ
προσευχῆς, f. 22v-53; Περὶ ἡσυχίας καὶ προσευχῆς, f. 78v-83; the Τύπον σύντομον
ἀσκητικῷ βίῳ κατάλληλον, f. 35v. This last work is to be found in *PG* 143, cols.
381-400; English translation (from the Russian) in Kadloubovsky and Palmer,
Writings from the Philokalia on Prayer of the Heart, pp. 383-94.

[9]*PG* 143, col. 393BC.

disciple's renown has eclipsed that of his master.[10] Gregory pursued the Hesychast life in various monastic centers on the Holy Mountain, as well as for a time on the nearby mountain of Beroea. When the Calabrian monk Barlaam began a campaign against the Hesychasts, attacking them as heretics, as Messalians, as ὀμφαλόψυχοι,[11] Gregory defended them and was henceforth involved in heated polemics. About 1341 the superiors and principal monks of Athos came out in support of Gregory in the document called the "Hagioritic Tome." The Council of St Sophia, under the presidency of the Emperor, condemned Barlaam (1341). Gregory was still to know strange and sudden changes of fortune. He was imprisoned, excommunicated, then raised to the Archbishopric of Thessalonica; he was later captured by Turkish corsairs and spent a year in custody. In 1368 his doctrine was declared the official teaching of the Byzantine Church. Already in 1351 the Council of Blachernae had incorporated in the Synodicon for the Sunday of Orthodoxy anathemas against Akyndinus, Nicephoros, Gregoras and other adversaries of Palamas. The latter was not only the author of countless controversial writings, such as the *Triads in Defense of the Holy Hesychasts,* but he is

---

[10]On Palamas, see M. Jugie, "Palamas" and "Palamite (controverse)", in *Dictionnaire de Théologie Catholique* 11 (1932), cols. 1735-1818. These articles are excellent in their positive part which contains texts and facts, but the interpretation given of these texts and facts has to be treated with serious reservations. The reader who wishes to follow the old adage *audiatur et altera pars* will find this *altera pars* in the work of G. Papamikhail, Ὁ ἅγιος Γρηγόριος Παλαμᾶς (Alexandria, 1911); in the study of Fr (Archbishop) Basil Krivosheine (Krivochéine), *The Ascetic and Theological Teaching of Gregory Palamas,* first published in English as a series of articles in *Eastern Churches Quarterly* III, 1-4 (1938), and then separately in a revised version (London, 1954); and in the books of Fr John Meyendorff, *A Study of Gregory Palamas* (Leighton Buzzard, 1964), and the more popular *St Gregory Palamas and Orthodox Spirituality* (Crestwood, 1974). See also the papers in the commemorative volume issued on the sixth centenary of Palamas' death, Πανηγυρικὸς Τόμος (Thessalonica, 1960). [For further bibliography, cf. Georgios I. Mantzaridis, *The Deification of Man: St Gregroy Palamas and the Orthodox Tradition* (Crestwood, 1984), pp. 131-3.]

[11]An ironic allusion, almost untranslatable, referring to the practice of those Hesychasts who, while pronouncing the Jesus Prayer, bowed their head and fixed their gaze on their navel or rather towards the middle of the body, in order to facilitate the "return of the intellect to the heart."

also the ascetical and mystical author of such works as
*Three Chapters on Prayer and Purity of Heart, On the
Passions and Virtues,* and *Decalogue of the Law according
to Christ.*[12]

Gregory did not discuss the Jesus Prayer specifically as
a topic on its own, but it is taken for granted in almost all
his writings, since he was replying to attacks directly aimed
against it. The most original and most controversial aspect
of his theology was his understanding of the "uncreated
light" and his distinction between the divine essence and
the divine energies. It was the Jesus Prayer that led Gregory
to develop these ideas, since the vision of the divine light,
of the "light of Tabor," was for Gregory the normal goal of
Hesychast prayer and of the invocation of the name. It was
in connection with these views of his on the uncreated light
that violent conflict developed. We shall not enter into this
controversy.[13] We shall say only this: there has been a
tendency to lose sight of the fact that the Hesychast theory
of the vision of the divine light is concerned with the

---

[12]A critical edition of Palamas' works is in progress under the general editorship
of Professor Panagiotis K. Christou (so far 3 vols.: Thessalonica, 1962-70). See also
the edition of the *Triads in Defense of the Holy Hesychasts* by John Meyendorff,
with critical Greek text and French translation *(Spicilegium Sacrum Lovaniense* 30-
31: 2 vols., Louvain, 1959; 2nd ed., Louvain, 1973); selections in English translation
are given in J. Meyendorff and N. Gendle, *Gregory Palamas: The Triads (The
Classics of Western Spirituality:* New York, 1983). For writings of Palamas not yet
included in the Thessalonica edition, see *PG* 150-151, and also the edition of twenty-
two *Homilies* by S. Oikonomos (Athens, 1861).

[13]Fr Jugie, in the two articles already cited from the *Dictionnaire de Théologie
Catholique,* discusses it in detail, from a Scholastic or more precisely an Aristotelian-
Thomistic point of view, not without a certain vehemence. The Orthodox Church's
understanding of the light of the Transfiguration is explained by Fr Georges
Florovsky, "The Mystery of the Light of Tabor" (in Russian), in *Feuillets de saint
Serge 3 (89) (Paris, 1935), and by Vladimir Lossky, In the Image and Likeness of
God* (Crestwood, 1974), pp.45-69. Consult, also by Lossky, *The Vision of God*
(London, 1963); [2nd ed., Crestwood, 1983]), and *The Mystical Theology of the
Eastern Church* (London, 1957; [reprint, Crestwood, 1976]). This last book, for all
its great merits, calls also for certain reservations. The reader insufficiently on his
guard is in danger of identifying Palamism with Orthodox spirituality as a whole,
and of underestimating the influence of the Desert Fathers, the Greek Fathers of the
4th century, and the oriental currents (Syrian, Egyptian, Armenian) outside the
sphere of Byzantium. Moreover, Lossky tends to overemphasize and harden
contrasts between East and West.

supernatural level and not with the normal psychological order; moreover, this controversy, like the *filioque* dispute, is the result largely of a misunderstanding between the two sides. We are in danger of creating monstrosities when we transpose a concept from one system of thought to another that is foreign to it, divorcing it from its context, and when we translate into certain intellectual categories ideas which can be conceived and expressed only in quite different categories.

Be that as it may, the fact remains that the Jesus Prayer was the more or less direct cause of the Palamite controversy and of the animosity thereby created between Greeks and Latins. This stream of simple and tender devotion expanded in the 14th century into an estuary of hostile quarrels. This was indeed deplorable. Monks who had learned to contemplate in peace launched into battle about the intellectual concepts in which their contemplation was expressed; as always, they became much less monks as a result. As for Gregory Palamas himself, he underwent the misfortune of all mystics who have interrupted their prayer so as to engage in disputes about it. It is true that he had been provoked by attacks which were often unjust and insulting. But would not the best response to the offensive directed against the Jesus Prayer have been the peaceful influence radiating from the Prayer itself, its deeper exploration and, if so desired, a brief testimony based on personal experience, free from theories and polemic? Whatever the gains for theological speculation from the Hesychast dispute—if anything was gained—for pure spirituality there was only loss.

Emerging from this conflict, it is refreshing to read a work as full of peace, devotion and a rare spiritual beauty as the *Century* of Kallistos and Ignatius Xanthopoulos.[14]

---

[14]*PG* 147, cols. 636-812; English translation (from the Russian) in Kadloubovsky and Palmer, *Writings from the Philokalia on Prayer of the Heart*, pp. 164-270. To our regret, we cannot agree with Fr V. Laurent about Kallistos and Ignatius. In his review of the present book (*Revue de Etudes byzantines* 17, p. 307), he writes that "the high value set on the *Century*" is "indefensible." While recognizing Fr Laurent's authority as a specialist in Byzantine studies, we venture to disagree with him here,

Both of them sought to remain above all monks and contemplatives. They were members of the Monastery of the Xanthopouloi in Constantinople. The Kallistos of the *Century* is the Patriarch of Constantinople, St Kallistos II, who occupied the patriarchal see in 1397 for three months only (not to be confused with his namesake Patriarch Kallistos I).

The *Century* constitutes a complete rule of life for the Hesychast. The center of this life is the Jesus Prayer. As regards technique, the *Century* recommends the formula, "Lord Jesus Christ, Son of God, have mercy on me." The authors distinguish here a twofold movement: a soaring ascent towards Jesus Christ in the first part of the prayer, "Lord Jesus Christ, Son of God. . ."; and a return to oneself, ". . . have mercy on me." The rhythm of the respiration is to be associated with this twofold movement.

---

since it is a matter not of establishing facts but of expressing a value-judgment.

Before taking literary leave of Fr Laurent, there is something more we have to say. He regards "this attractive little book" (our own), despite its "shadows," as "a valuable outline of a major theme." We thank him sincerely for this estimate (doubtless too complimentary). But when he goes on to speak of the "indictment" that we bring against "Catholic theologians," we venture to make a respectful but pained protest. Far be it from us to bring an indictment against anyone! Our intention—and of this we can speak with certainty—has been in no way polemical. No more (so we hope) was our manner of writing. The meticulous reader who compares the 1963 edition with its predecessor will find that, in the case of certain modern writers, we have actually omitted various quotations from them, even though these were exact, and have toned down various comments on them, even though these could be justified. We have written in an eirenic spirit. It has been, and continues to be, our hope that we have contributed to a *rapprochement* on the level of spirituality.

[David Balfour, *Saint Gregory the Sinaïte: Discourse on the Transfiguration*, p. 147, draws attention to an unpublished text (Bodleian Holkham gr. 74, ff. 131r-133r), in which Kallistos and Ignatius recommend the use of the short formula "My Jesus" to those who find themselves unable to recite the full text of the Prayer: "The divine energy wells up from the heart, snatching up, as it were, the affection of the heart and stirring the intellect from the very depths. It becomes so attached to the divine energy itself, that it cries out repeatedly, 'My Jesus, my Jesus! ('Ιησοῦ μου).' For as soon as the heart is opened up, this is all that the intellect cries out: 'My Jesus!', and the intellect is incapable of saying the whole formula, 'Lord Jesus Christ, Son of God, have mercy on me', because of the frequent openings of the heart; but it can only say 'My Jesus!' " This is closely parallel to what is said in Russian nineteenth century texts (see below, pp. 78 and 83, note 2), and confirms Fr Lev's advice about the recitation of the name of Jesus on its own.]

This practice produces a certain warmth in the heart.

What is more important is that the *Century* inserts the Jesus Prayer into a general ascetic context. It takes the Hesychast by the hand and guides him from dawn to dusk. It lays down as a fundamental principle that there can be no *hesychia* without Orthodox faith and good works; the danger of quietism is thus eliminated. Next come precise, practical directions: about silence, the reading of Scripture, nightly vigils, prostrations (300 a day), fasting (a diet of dry vegetables, bread and water; wine is sometimes allowed), communion "with a pure heart," psalmody for those who are not yet capable of concentrating on the Jesus Prayer. Throughout these detailed recommendations the spiritual goal is always kept in view. The aim is to attain a state in which the soul devoted to the Jesus Prayer can say with the Song of Songs, "I am wounded with love" (5:8). The *Century* remains a precious manual. Even today, to those called by God to adopt the Prayer as their own particular path and in a position to organize their life around it, one cannot recommend a better guide—with some necessary adaptations—or at least a better initiation.

From Mount Athos the Jesus Prayer spread not only throughout the Greek East but also to the Slav world. By the first half of the 15th century, if not before, it was being practiced in Russia. The Jesus Prayer is mentioned in an instruction for the training of young novices, dating from this period and emanating from the Monastery of the Trinity near Obnora, founded in 1389 by Paul, disciple of St Sergius of Radonezh. It is supposed to be said on the beads of the monastic rosary or prayer-rope. St Nil Sorsky (Nil Maikov, 1433-1508), who had lived on Athos and came under the influence of Gregory the Sinaite, propagated the Jesus Prayer among the "monks across the Volga." In his works he presents it as an ascetic task, a "labor," and "action," and this way of conceiving it has never disappeared from Russian monasticism. The spiritual movement of the "Transvolga" monks, so deeply opposed to the institutionalism which was to prevail in the Russian Church, had a natural affinity with Hesychasm and with the tendencies represented by the Jesus Prayer.[15] In the 16th century we find the Prayer well established in Russia.[16] In the 17th century the Jesus Prayer was advocated by St Dimitri, Metropolitan of Rostov (1651-1709), who was not only a dogmatic theologian and a catechetical writer but author of the works *Spiritual Medicine* (on the ways of freeing oneself from evil thoughts) and *The Interior Man* (on the effectiveness of prayer). It is interesting that Dimitri was at the same time a latinizer and that he accepted the views of Roman theologians on the Immaculate Conception of Mary and on the eucharistic epiclesis.[17]

[15]A. Arkhangelskii, *Nil Sorsky and Cassian Patrikiev. Their Literary Works and their Ideas in Ancient Russia* (in Russian) (St Petersburg, 1882). [See also G.A. Maloney, *Russian Hesychasm. The Spirituality of Nil Sorskij* (The Hague /Paris, 1973), especially pp. 134-44, 269-79.]

On Russian spirituality in general, see Pierre Kovalevsky, *St Sergius and Russian Spirituality* (Crestwood, 1976); I. Kologrivov, *Essai sur la sainteté en Russie* (Bruges, 1953); and above all I. Smolitsch, *Moines de la sainte Russie* (Paris, 1967). [Cf. also G.P. Fedotov, *A Treasury of Russian Spirituality* (London, 1950); *The Russian Religious Mind* (2 vols.: Cambridge, Mass., 1946, 1966); E. Behr-Sigel, *Prière et sainteté dans l'Eglise russe* (Paris, 1950: revised ed., Bellefontaine, 1982).]

[16]A.S. Orlov, *The Prayer of Jesus in Russia in the Sixteenth Century* (in Russian), in the Russian collection *Monuments of Ancient Literature* (1914), no. 185.

[17]As far as we know the last work to appear on Dimitri is that of Popov, *St Dimitri of Rostov and his Works* (in Russian) (St Petersburg, 1910). For extracts from his writings, see S. Tyszkiewicz and Th. Belpaire, *Ascètes russes* (Namur, 1957), pp. 18-30.

CHAPTER IV

THE AGE OF THE PHILOKALIA

Since the Palamite controversy Mount Athos has not played a particularly active role in the development of Hesychast prayer. In the 18th century, however, the Holy Mountain did once again become the center of an intense diffusion of the Jesus Prayer. This was due to the work of two spiritual guides whose names cannot be separated: St Macarius of Corinth and St Nicodemus of the Holy Mountain.

Metropolitan Macarius of Corinth (1731-1805) had been deprived of his bishopric under Turkish pressure and reduced to a more or less wandering life. He died as a hermit on Chios.[1] He caused a certain amount of scandal by publishing anonymously in Venice, in 1777, an *Encheiridion* on "participation in the divine mysteries"; in this work he upheld the practice of frequent communion, at that time considered a Latin custom.[2] During the course of the same year he made his first journey to Mount Athos and there he met Nicodemus of Naxos, known as "the Hagiorite," that is, "of the Holy Mountain." A canonist, who played a predominant part in editing the *Pedalion*, a hagiographer, a liturgist, an ascetical and mystical writer, Nico-

---

[1]The life of Macarius was written by his disciple Athanasius of Paros and can be found in an abridged form in the hagiographical collection Νέον Λειμονάριον, published in Venice in 1819 by another of Macarius' disciples, Nicephoros of Chios, and re-edited in Chios in 1913. See the article on Macarius by L. Petit in *Dictionnaire de théologie catholique* 9 (1927), cols. 1449-52; cf. M.J. le Guillou, "La renaissance spirituelle du XVIIIe siècle," in *Istina* 7 (1960), pp. 95-128. [See also C. Cavarnos, *St Macarius of Corinth* (Belmont, Mass., 1972); D. Stiernon, in *Dictionnaire de Spiritualité* 10 (1977), cols. 10-11.]

[2]This book is extremely rare. In recent times only two copies of it have been known to exist: one at the Athonite monastery of Xeropotamou and another in the possession of Msgr L. Petit, Latin Archbishop of Athens.

demus (1749-1809) has an equal claim with Evgenios Boulgaris (1716-1806) to be regarded as the greatest Greek religious writer of the 18th century; and there is no doubt that
he was spiritually far superior to Boulgaris.

Nicodemus shared with Macarius a sympathetic attitude
towards certain notions prevailing in the Latin West. He
translated into Greek (1796) the *Spiritual Combat* of the
Theatine Lorenzo Scupoli, and in 1800 he even published
Spiritual Exercises based closely on those of St Ignatius,
comprising thirty-four meditations, each in three points.[3] He
shared Macarius' opinion about frequent communion and
helped the holy bishop to revise his book of 1777, the result
of this collaboration being the publication in Venice, in
1783, of another anonymous work entitled *A Book Very
Useful for the Soul on Worthy Participation in the Most
Pure Mysteries of Christ;* this is Macarius' book, but adapted
by Nicodemus with new developments. The work was at
first prohibited by the Patriarch of Constantinople, but
when the monks of Athos expressed support for it the
condemnation was rescinded. Macarius did not settle per-
manently on Athos; after his first visit in 1777, he did not
return again until 1784. As a matter of fact the book of
1783 was only a minor publication by the two writers. It
was in the preceding year that the major work of Macarius
and Nicodemus appeared: the *Philokalia.*

The word φιλοκαλία means "love of beauty," but this
term must be understood according to the Hellenistic approach which identifies the beautiful and the good; it is a
question here of spiritual beauty. There exists a selection
from Origen's works under this title. Macarius wanted to
compose an anthology of Hesychasm, more specifically of
Hesychast prayer and the Jesus Prayer. Nicodemus was

---

[3]M. Viller, "Nicodème l'Hagiorite et ses emprunts à la littérature spirituelle
occidentale," in *Revue d'Ascétique et de mystique* 5 (1924), pp. 174-7. The life of
Nicodemus was written by one of his contemporaries, the priest-monk Evthymios;
the text has been published in Γρηγόριος ὁ Παλαμᾶς 4 (1920), pp. 636-41, and 5
(1921), pp. 210-18. Cf. C. Papoulidis, *Nicodème l'Hagiorite (1749-1809)* (Athens,
1967); [C. Cavarnos, *St. Nicodemos the Hagiorite* (Belmont, 1974); D. Stiernon, in
Dictionnaire de spiritualité 11 (1981), cols. 234-50.]

already attracted by similar ideas. He admired Symeon the New Theologian, whose works he translated and edited in the Greek vernacular in collaboration with Denis Zagoraios (Venice, 1790). He also prepared an edition of the letters of Barsanuphius and John, published only after his death (Vienna, 1816). He was therefore inwardly well prepared for this undertaking, in which, however, it was Macarius who took the initiative. The respective parts played by the two in the composition of the *Philokalia* cannot be determined with any precision; all that one can say is that their collaboration was very close. It resulted in a work of considerable dimensions,[4] in which were gathered together the most significant texts relating to Hesychast life and above all to the Jesus Prayer, not only from the writers whom we have ourselves quoted in this book, but from a number of others as well. The reader will appreciate the importance of the *Philokalia* for our subject if we say that the work of Macarius and Nicodemus constitutes a "Summa of the Jesus Prayer."

*

* *

Nicodemus of the Holy Mountain also wrote an original work on Hesychast prayer entitled *A Manual of Counsel on the Guarding of the Five Senses, of the Imag-*

---

[4]The Φιλοκαλία τῶν ἱερῶν νηπτικῶν (the complete Greek title comprises no less than 28 words) was published anonymously in Venice in 1782, at the expense of the Greek philanthropist John Mavrocordato. This *editio princeps* has 1207 in-folio pages. It is very rare: of all the German and Austrian libraries, only that of Göttingen University possesses a copy of it. We have before us the 1782 edition which belongs to the British Museum. It is divided into two parts. The first contains writings by (or attributed to) Antony the Great, Isaias, Evagrius, Cassian, Mark, Hesychius, Nilus, Diadochus, John of Carpathus, Theodore, Maximus, Thalassius, John Damascene, Philemon, Theognostus, Philotheus the Sinaite, Elias, Theophanes. The second part contains works by or concerning Peter of Damascus, Symeon Metaphrastes, Symeon the New Theologian, Nicetas Stethatos, Theoleptus, Nicephorus, Gregory the Sinaite, Gregory Palamas (including the Hagioritic Tome), Kallistos and Ignatius Xanthopoulos, Kallistos the Patriarch, Kallistos Angelikoudes, Kallistos Kataphygiotes, Symeon of Thessalonica, Mark of Ephesus, Maximus of Kapsokalyvia. It

ination, of the Intellect and of the Heart.[5] The author gives
some very definite advice on the Jesus Prayer (ch. 10). In
this chapter we read: "Beginners customarily bring about
this return of the intellect *(nous)* to the heart, as our holy
ascetic Fathers have taught, by bowing their heads and by
resting their beards on the top of their chests." The disciple
is told to hold his breath momentarily, because this helps to
control the dispersion and dissipation of the intellect. He is
to practice this control of the breathing in the evening, for
one or two hours without interruption, in a dark and quiet
place. In this way the intellect "is gathered together and
returns to the heart." There it finds the "inner discourse"
(ἐνδιάθετος λόγος); and it is this interior voice that recites
the Jesus Prayer. "Therefore let your intellect, having once
discovered this inner discourse, not allow it to say anything
but the short prayer called 'monologic': *Lord Jesus Christ,
Son of God, have mercy on me.*" There must be nothing
mechanical about the Jesus Prayer; it must be placed in its
full spiritual context. "This prayer alone is not sufficient.
One must also set into motion the soul's will-power; the
soul must say this prayer with all its will, all its strength
and all its love." We are to avoid all imagination, every
"impression of a form, whatever it may be," and to remember the advice of St Nilus (i.e., Evagrius): "Approach
the Immaterial in an immaterial way."

  This work by Nicodemus will seem disconcerting to the
Western reader, because of the way in which it combines a
particular physical technique with a spirituality of profound

---

seems that, when publishing the *Patrologia Graeca*, Migne (or more precisely Dom
Pitra) did not learn about the *Philokalia* and employ it until a relatively late point;
frequent use of the texts and biographical notices in the *Philokalia* is made only
from *PG* 147, col. 634 onwards. [For the first mention of the *Philokalia*, see *PG* 85,
col. 791.] On the publication of the *Philokalia*, see E. Legrand, L. Petit and H.
Pernod, *Bibliographie Hellénique du XVIII*e *siècle*, vol. 2 (Paris, 1929), pp. 391-4.
[Cf. C. Cavarnos, *Byzantine Thought and Art* (2nd ed., Belmont, Mass, 1974), pp.
48-58; K. Ware, in *Dictionnaire de spiritualité* 12 (1984), cols. 1336-52.]

  [5]This Ἐγχειρίδιον συμβουλευτικόν appeared in 1801, with no indication of the
place of publication; it was reissued in Athens in 1885, and in Volos in 1958. For
extracts in French translation, see J. Gouillard, *Petite Philocalie de la prière du
coeur* (Paris, 1953), pp. 310-16; [in English translation, see C. Cavarnos, *St Nicodemos the Hagiorite*, pp. 142-5.]

self-stripping and interiorization. His astonishment (shall we say his embarrassment?) will increase, when, on page 328 of the 1801 edition which we have before us, he looks at the anatomical diagrams of the human heart, drawn in the most precise and scientific manner. Here, then, at the beginning of the 19th century, is a writer with an exceptional literary and theological background, with an authentic and deep spiritual experience, who is well-informed about the theories of the anatomists and physiologists of his time; and yet he does not hesitate to recommend psycho-physiological methods of prayer, worked out in the Byzantine Middle Ages by monks whose notions on breathing, on the heart and the brain are bound to seem somewhat primitive. Since Nicodemus is historically the last of the Hesychasts—which, as we shall see, does not mean that the history of the Jesus Prayer ended with him—perhaps it will be useful to pause for a moment and to look more closely at the Jesus Prayer as he himself describes it, faithfully reflecting a long tradition.

Invariably and essentially, the Jesus Prayer consists in a formula in which the name of Jesus is invoked. In the second place, according to many authors it also involves a physical method designed to facilitate the recitation of the formula. Let us consider first of all the formula itself.

The formula, as it exists in modern monastic usage, is: "Lord Jesus Christ, Son of God, have mercy on me a sinner." The words "a sinner" are lacking the formula indicated by Nicodemus, but his formula already implies it to a certain degree. The modern formula combines two Gospel prayers, in a modified form: the cry of the two blind men, "Son of David, have mercy on us" (Mt 9:27); and the humble request of the Publican, "God, have mercy on me a sinner" (Lk 18:13). The element that the two prayers share in common is "have mercy." The prayer of the two blind men supplies the vocative "Son. . .," but "Son of David" is replaced by "Son of God."

This phrase is preceded by the words "Lord Jesus Christ." These three words are found combined for the first

time in Acts 16:31: "Believe in the Lord Jesus Christ." The
juxtaposition of the two words "Jesus" and "Christ" is already a confession of faith. The first of these words, from
an etymological point of view, implies that there is in the
name of Jesus a σωτηρία, a mystery of salvation, and in the
person of Jesus the presence of God's saving power. The
second word ascribes to Jesus Messianic anointing, both
priestly and royal. The word "Lord" confesses Jesus' "lord-
ship," and this term had a particularly strong meaning in
the first century, when emperor-worship tended to mono-
polize its use in an idolatrous way. Its employment by the
Christians met therefore with vehement opposition.[6] The
transition from "Lord Jesus Christ" to "Son of God"—
another very explicit confession of faith—was perhaps suggested by the high priest's words: ". . .if thou be the Christ,
the Son of God" (Mt 26:63).

The phrase "have mercy" is generally expressed by the
Greek ἐλέησον, which is the term used by the two blind
men in the Gospel of Matthew. But sometimes in the Jesus
Prayer, instead of ἐλέησον the word ἱλάσθητι is used,
which Luke puts on the Publican's lips. The difference in
meaning between the two terms is considerable. The words
ἔλεος, "mercy," ἐλεέω, "I show mercy," and ἐλεημοσύνη,
"almsgiving," all alike express the common notion of compassionate mercy, expressed through loving self-abasement.
One finds the same idea in the Slavonic words milost',
milostiv, pomilovat', pomilui, used in the Slavonic versions
of the Jesus Prayer; here, however, there is also a special
nuance which might be expressed by the word benignity.
But ἱλάσθητι says something else. The verb ἱλάσκομαι
implies the idea of appeasing, reconciliation, propitiation;
the same sense is found also in the words ἱλασμός, ἱλαστή-
ριος, ἱλαστήριον. One may recall that this last word designates, in the Greek Bible, the "propitiation" or "mercy-seat"
which covered the Ark and which the Book of Exodus

---

[6]W. Bousset, Kyrios Christos. Geschichte des Christusglaubens von den Anfängen
des Christentums bis Irenaeus (Göttingen, 1913).

describes (25:17-22; cf. Heb 9:5). This strong meaning did not exist originally in, for example, the Homeric term ἵλαος, "goodness," "grace," or in ἱλαρός, "joyful," from which is derived our word "hilarious"; but by degrees it came to be more accentuated, so that the Publican's prayer should be translated "be propitious to me" rather than "have mercy on me." If, then, in the Jesus Prayer, one uses ἱλάσθητι instead of ἐλέησον, this introduces into it the notion of the mystery of redemption and of all that the Germans understand by *Versöhnung* and the English by *Atonement*. The Greek text of the Liturgy juxtaposes the two verbs in the prayer that the priest says at the prothesis: Ὁ Θεός ἱλάσθητι μοι τῷ ἁμαρτωλῷ καί ἐλέησόν με, "God, be propitious to me a sinner and have mercy on me." The Slavonic text translates very accurately: "God, purify *(otchisti)* me a sinner and have mercy on me." The liturgical *Kyrie eleison* has probably also had an influence upon the Jesus Prayer; there is no record of it earlier than Book VIII of the *Apostolic Constitutions*,[7] and it appeared about the middle of the 4th century. The fact that it first emerges in the region of Antioch suggests that it may have been used in the monastic deserts of Syria.

From all this it is clear that there exists, beneath the very simple formula of the Jesus Prayer, an extremely rich theology. Far from being monotonous, this prayer contains a wonderful diversity, if the person making use of it emphasizes in turn, according to his particular needs or the grace given to him, the various aspects of the formula. Nevertheless it must be remembered that the name of Jesus suffices by itself to constitute the Jesus Prayer. It was only after many centuries, during which the Prayer had an undefined and fluid character, that a fairly fixed and rigid form came to be imposed upon it. But he who wishes to return to the primitive freedom and to concentrate on the name alone, abandoning the developed formula, is fully entitled to claim that he is practicing the Jesus Prayer. For

---

[7] F.E. Brightman, *Liturgies Eastern and Western* (Oxford, 1896), pp. 4-5.

he is in fact returning to the earliest historical usage of the
Prayer, and is restoring to the term *monologistos* its literal
meaning, "a prayer consisting of a single word," the single
word that is the Word himself in the absolute sense and
that the Father utters eternally.

Since the Middle Ages the monks of the Byzantine East
have associated the recitation of the Jesus Prayer with the
use of a rosary or prayer-rope which helps in counting the
invocations. This rosary is given to the monks and nuns during the ceremony of monastic profession. The recitation of
the Jesus Prayer or, in other words, of a certain number of
rosaries—accompanied by "metanoias," prostrations or
bows—can replace whole or part of the divine office according to a table of clearly defined equivalents. In this
way the Jesus Prayer is something more than a private
devotion. To some extent it forms a part of the canonical
prayer of the Church, and indeed is prescribed by the 87th
rule of the *Nomocanon*.[8].

---

[8]The Greeks call the monastic rosary κομβοσχοίνιον, the Russians *lestovka*,
vervitsa, or *tchotki*. The Greek rosary is made up of 100 pearls or wooden beads or
knots of wool or thread. The practice is to make one rosary bead and one metanoia
correspond to each Jesus Prayer. There are two kinds of metanoia: the lesser
metanoia, a deep bow without bending the knees; and the greater metanoia or full
prostration, with the forehead touching the ground. On Mount Athos, 1,200 (12 x
100) greater metanoias are made every day, and in the evening 300 lesser metanoias.
The Jesus Prayer has two forms. The ordinary one is very full: "Lord Jesus Christ,
Son and Word of the living God, through the prayers of thy most pure Mother and
of all the Saints, have mercy on us and save us." The shorter form, "Lord Jesus
Christ, Son of God, have mercy on me," is considered a penitential prayer. The
Russian usages are different. The Russian rosary is composed of 107 knots divided
in this way: 1 large knot and 17 small knots, 2 large knots and 33 small knots, 1 large
knot and 40 small knots, 1 large knot and 12 small knots. These four divisions
represent the four parts of the daily office: Vespers, Compline, Matins, and the
prayers called "Typika." The Russians use the formula: "Lord Jesus Christ, Son of
God, have mercy on us." They make fewer metanoias than the Greeks. In their use
of the rosary, they begin with 10 greater metanoias, next 30 lesser metanoias (both
accompanied by the Jesus Prayer); then the Jesus Prayer is said 60 times without
metanoias; on the remaining knots great metanoias are made. The rosary should be
said 5 times a day. The Russian equivalents between the Jesus Prayer (with
metanoias at each invocation) and the office are: for Vespers, 500; for Compline,
200; for Matins, 500; for the Typika, 700. One sees that the practice is somewhat
severe. See A. Maltzew, *Andachtsbuch der Orthodox-Katholischen Kirche des
Morgenlandes* (Berlin, 1895), pp. civ-cx. We cannot say to what extent the Uniate

Let us pass now from the formula to the physical methods which have become associated with it. We have noted that the Athonite Hesychasts linked to the Jesus Prayer certain practices or experiences—retention of the breathing, fixing the gaze on the middle of the body, perception of a light—which may shock or at least surprise us. We shall make only two observations on this subject.

First of all, one must be very prudent, very guarded, when speaking of a method which one views from the outside and has not experienced personally. It is easy for Latin writers to speak ironically about the Hesychast technique or to be scandalized by it. Of this technique they know only what they have read. Those who have practical knowledge of Hesychast methods—and such persons still exist in our time—no longer write about this subject. But one cannot disapprove *a priori* of someone who tries to find bodily dispositions capable of making prayer easier. St Ignatius Loyola, in his *Spiritual Exercises,* attached considerable importance to the outward setting and the bodily attitude of the person performing the exercises. This is only natural and legitimate. An Oriental Christian who mocked or criticized the Latins for making genuflections and sometimes praying with arms outstretched in the form of a cross would be showing particularly bad taste. When a tradition of prayer, like that of Athos, is many centuries old, when generations of ascetics and mystics whose testimony is not to be lightly rejected have believed that certain methods help their prayer, it would be only wise to ask oneself whether, after all, there is not something positive in these methods. Here as always, a certain respectful reserve is appropriate, especially among those who belong to a dif-

monks practice the Jesus Prayer. It was in use among the Studites of Oriental Galicia, who are now dispersed, but we do not know what is the practice among the Ruthenian Basilians, the Italo-Greeks and Syrians. Among Uniate secular priests and lay people, the Latin rosary has, we believe, to a considerable degree replaced the Jesus Prayer.

[The Orthodox prayer rope can also take a number of forms not indicated above. It may have less or more than 100 knots, and the knots are often differently subdivided, for example in groups of 10 or 25.]

ferent tradition.[9]

Having said this, it is important to make a clear distinction between the Jesus Prayer and all forms of psychophysiological technique. The invocation of the name of Jesus is sufficient by itself. Its best supports are of a spiritual and moral order. Moreover, none of the followers of the Athonite technique has ever maintained that this technique is essential to the Jesus Prayer. Today, indeed, when one of the faithful after reading texts from the past is tempted to adopt the Hesychast technique, the general practice of Orthodox spiritual directors is to dissuade him or her from doing so. For most people such attempts would be useless and dangerous, even though, in certain cases under the guidance of experienced directors, they might bear fruit. The Christian attracted by the Jesus Prayer and starting out on this particular spiritual way would therefore do well to disregard the psycho-physiological methods recommended by the monks of the past. Let him say to himself quite simply that these things, which may be excellent in a certain *milieu* and in specific circumstances, have not been written for him. The path of the psychosomatic methods is not closed to those who would set out on it with necessary prudence and under reliable guidance. But every Christian can attain to the summits of the Jesus Prayer with no other "technique" except that of love and obedience. It is the inner attitude that is here all-important. The Jesus Prayer confers upon us freedom from everything except Jesus himself.

*

*   *

What has just been said might seem self-evident. There is, however, a real danger of falling into strange misapprehensions about this subject. It would be a grave misunder-

---

[9]Cf. Appendix I.

standing of the historical evidence to see in the Jesus Prayer a more or less exterior method, a "recipe" dispensing us from serious moral effort.[10] This would be to forget all that the Hesychasts have written about "guarding the heart" as an indispensable condition for the Jesus Prayer. They never saw in the Prayer a "short way" to avoid the renunciation which the royal road of the Holy Cross demands from us. What distinguished them from "asceticism" pure and simple was their belief that it was the Jesus Prayer that led them to these renunciations and that rendered them easier to bear and less harsh; but they did not imagine that the Jesus Prayer could exist without νῆψις or "sobriety." This Greek word implies that total vigilant control of oneself which is also expressed by the term "asceticism." "Sobriety and prayer are united as soul and body; if one of them is lacking, the other cannot stand firm." This statement is made at the very beginning of the *Method of Holy Prayer and Attention*, the primary manual of Hesychasm.

The Hesychast understanding of the relationship between prayer and asceticism has never been better expressed than by the Studite monk Nicetas Stethatos, the biographer and devoted admirer of Symeon the New Theologian, in his *Centuries*.[11] He says that man's return to the original divine image demands a reshaping of our senses and their reordering once more under the guidance of the intellect *(nous)*. The external senses should receive only the *logoi* or essential impressions of things; they must be dematerialized and should render the irrational submissive to that which is intelligible: the sense of taste is to be directed by the discernment of the reason, the sense of hearing by the

---

[10]We agree with Fr Hausherr when he writes: "Strange though these methods may be, they are not altogether the exclusive property of Orientals and undoubtedly the well-informed theologian will not deny *a priori* their legitimacy. He will require only that one should not attribute to them an infallible efficacy, and especially that one should not hope thereby to attain divine contemplation without passing through all the ascetic renunciations and purifications." ("A propos de spiritualité hésychaste," in *Orientalia Christiana Periodica* 3 [Rome, 1937], p. 271; reprinted in *Hésychasme et prière*, p. 61.)

[11]*PG* 120, cols. 852-1009; cf. Nicetas Stethatos, *Opuscules et lettres*, ed. J. Darrouzès (*Sources chrétiennes* 81: Paris, 1961).

soul's understanding, and so on with all the five senses. We
are brought back from carnal satisfaction to higher ends.
Such is the high asceticism that Hesychasm recommends.
How, then, can it be considered an easy system? Furthermore, neither the disciples of the New Theologian nor the
monks of Athos were ever in danger of forgetting the
crucial importance of the "spiritual father" whose guidance
protects the beginner against self-indulgence and illusion.
The same Nicetas wrote: "Not to submit oneself to a spiritual father, in imitation of the Son who was obedient to his
Father even to death on the Cross, is not to be born from
above."[12] Therefore let no one speak of mechanical methods
or of a "short way." The Jesus Prayer is a book to be
opened and read only in an evangelical spirit of humble
love and self-giving.

*

* *

Having, as we hope, to some extent cleared the atmosphere, let us return to the history of the Jesus Prayer.
Paissy Velichkovsky (1722-94), of Russian origin, was the
apostle of the Jesus Prayer in Romania, where he directed
the monastery of Niamets. One of the great names in
Orthodox monastic history, he had lived for a time on
Athos. He translated the *Philokalia* into Church Slavonic
under the title *Dobrotolubie* ("love of the beautiful" becomes in Slavonic "love of the good"). The *Dobrotolubie*[13]
had an even greater influence upon the Russian people than

---

[12]*Chapters* II, 54 (col. 925B).
[13]The work, comprising three parts, appeared in Moscow in 1793. This edition is
very rare outside Russia, but there is a copy in the British Museum. Of the 36 texts in
the Greek *Philokalia*, only 24 were included by Paissy. See further "Un Moine de
l'Eglise orthodoxe de Roumanie" (Fr André Scrima), "L'avènement philocalique
dans l'Orthodoxie roumaine," *Istina* 5 (1958), pp. 295-328, 443-74. [Cf. *Blessed
Paisius Velichkovsky*, ed. St Herman of Alaska Brotherhood (Platina, 1976); Sergii
Chetverikov, *Starets Paissii Velichkovskii* (Belmont, Mass., 1980).]

the *Philokalia* has had upon the Greeks. It was through this collection of texts that not only monks but simple village people became familiar with the Fathers and with the Jesus Prayer. Paissy also wrote a letter to the "enemies and slanderers of the Jesus Prayer." In this he says: "One should know that this divine action was the constant occupation of our fathers who were filled with God. It shone as a sun in many places, in the desert and in cenobitic monasteries: on Sinai, in the sketes of Egypt, on Mount Nitria, in Jerusalem and in the neighboring monasteries, in a word in the whole of the East and later in Constantinople, on the Holy Mountain of Athos, on many islands, and in these last times, through the grace of Christ, also in Russia."[14]

St Seraphim of Sarov (1759-1833), the most popular of modern Russian saints, did not insist in a particular way on the Jesus Prayer. It might be said that he had a soul that was above all Pentecostal, and that he concentrated his spiritual life on the "acquisition of the Holy Spirit." This will be obvious to readers of his famous *Conversation with Motovilov*. Yet he also wrote the following lines: "In order to receive and feel Christ's light in the heart, one must withdraw as much as possible from all visible things. When the soul, with inner faith in the Crucified, has purified itself by repentance and good works, one must close the eyes of the body, make the understanding descend into the heart, and call unceasingly upon the name of our Lord Jesus Christ: 'Lord Jesus Christ, Son of God, have mercy on me.' Then a person, according to the measure of his zeal and fervor towards the Beloved, finds in the invocation of the name consolation and sweetness, and this arouses in him the desire to seek higher illumination."[15] It is also noteworthy that one of the earliest biographies of Seraphim

---

[14]For extracts from this letter, see Chetverikov, pp. 178-220.

[15]These lines are found, not in the *Conversation with Motovilov*, but in the few written fragments left by Seraphim. The English work by A.F. Dobbie-Bateman, *St. Seraphim of Sarov. Concerning the Aim of the Christian Life* (London, 1936), seems to us the best introduction to Seraphim's life and spirituality. The *Conversation with Motovilov* is translated in it. See also Irina Goraïnoff, *Séraphim de Sarov. Sa Vie*, followed by the *Conversation with Motovilov* and the *Spiritual*

contains a long supplement on the Jesus Prayer.[16] Included
in this are some very interesting reflections on the return of
the spirit to the heart, on the sensation of warmth which is
then produced, and on the transition from the "complete
prayer" ("Lord Jesus Christ, Son of God, have mercy on
me") to this simple cry: *Iissousse moi!* "My Jesus!"

A leading Russian spiritual teacher of the last century,
Ignatius Brianchaninov (1807-1867), Bishop of Kostroma, devoted one of his works to the Jesus Prayer.[17] He also
published an edition of the *Dobrotolubie*[18] more complete
than that of Paissy. The history of the Jesus Prayer in the
19th century is linked to a great extent with the history of
the *Dobrotolubie* or of the *Philokalia*. Another famous Russian ascetic, Theophan Govorov (1815-1894), called Theophan the Recluse, Bishop of Tambov, then of Vladimir,
who finally retired to the "desert" of Vyshen, prepared a
new edition of the *Dobrotolubie*, considerably larger than
the earlier editions, and this was reissued several times.[19] In
this edition a sharp distinction is made between the Jesus
Prayer as such and the psycho-physiological techniques.
Theophan states that he has omitted "certain external methods which scandalize some and lead them to abandon the
practice of the Prayer, while in the case of others they
deform the practice of the Prayer itself." These methods
are only "external preparations for interior activity, without
contributing anything essential to it." This advice follows:
"It must be remembered that, on our side, there is only the

Instructions (Bellefontaine, 1973); [Valentine Zander, *St Seraphim of Sarov* (Crestwood, 1975); C. Cavarnos and M.-B. Zeldin, *St. Seraphim of Sarov* (Belmont, Mass.,
1980).]

[16]*Accounts of the Life and Ascetic Exploits of our Father Seraphim* (in Russian)
(Moscow, 1855). The supplement to which we refer has no less than 79 pages.

[17]*On the Prayer of Jesus* (in Russian) (St Petersburg, 1865); English translation by
Fr Lazarus (London, 1952; reprinted London, 1965). [Cf. E. Simonod, *La Prière de
Jésus selon l'évêque Ignace Briantchaninoff (1807-1867)* (Paris, 1976).]

[18]St Petersburg, 1857. Paissy's *Dobrotolubie* was re-edited in two parts: one part
in 1853, the other in 1855.

[19]This edition, in five large volumes (1877-89; the index was issued separately in
1905), was published at Moscow for the Russian monastery of St Panteleimon on
Mount Athos.

effort, while the reality itself, namely the union of the intellect with the heart, is a gift of grace granted when and as the Lord wills. . .The essence of the practice [of the Jesus Prayer] consists in acquiring the habit of keeping the intellect on guard within the heart. . .within this physical heart, although not in a physical way."[20] Theophan's edition is in Russian; but a re-edition of the *Dobrotolubie* in Church Slavonic was published at the beginning of the 20th century.[21] The Greeks, for their part, have several times re-edited the *Philokalia*.[22]

---

[20]*Dobrotolubie*, vol. 5 (Moscow, 1889), pp. 469-70. The last sentence quoted requires a careful commentary; this effort of calm, slow descent, leading to an inhabitation of the intellect within the heart, is an experience which is very real, but which it is useless to try to describe on paper. But one can in any case appreciate how the entire question has been reconsidered even on Mount Athos itself.

[21]Synodal typography, Moscow, 1902. To our knowledge this edition is obtainable, outside of Russia and Athos, only at the library of the University of Helsinki.

[22]A slightly expanded edition appeared in two volumes at Athens in 1893; a further edition in five volumes was issued by the publishing house "Astir", Athens, in 1957-63, and this was reprinted at Athens in 1974-76. In English, see the partial translation of the *Philokalia* in two volumes, based on Theophan's Russian text, by E. Kadloubovsky and G.E.H. Palmer, *Writings from the Philokalia on Prayer of the Heart* (London, 1951), and *Early Fathers from the Philokalia* (London, 1954). [A full translation of the Greek edition is now in progress, translated by G.E.H. Palmer, P. Sherrard and K. Ware, *The Philokalia*, vol. 1 (London, 1979); vol. 2 (London, 1981); vol. 3 (London, 1984); two further vols. to follow.] In French, see J. Gouillard, *Petite Philocalie de la prière du coeur* (Paris, 1953; 2nd ed., Paris, 1968).

CHAPTER V

THE WAY OF A PILGRIM
AND THE JESUS PRAYER IN OUR AGE

A small book entitled *Sincere Tales of a Pilgrim to His Spiritual Father* appeared in Kazan in 1884.[1] To English readers it is generally known as *The Way of a Pilgrim*. It had been copied by Fr Paissy (†1883), Abbot of the monastery of St Michael of the Cheremissi in Kazan, from a manuscript in the possession of an Athonite monk. Judging from certain allusions made by the anonymous author, it was probably written after the Crimean war and before the abolition of Russian serfdom, that is, between 1855 and 1861. The "pilgrim" *(strannik)* describes the odyssey across Russia which he made with a knapsack containing dry bread and a Bible. In one monastery he meets a *starets* (spiritual father) and asks him how to carry out the Apostle's advice: "Pray without ceasing" (1 Thess 5:17). The *starets* puts the *Dobrotolubie* into the pilgrim's hands and explains to him the practice of the Jesus Prayer. He subjects him to what may be termed a regime of progressive training. He has him say the Jesus Prayer at first 3,000 times a day, then 6,000 times, and finally 12,000 times. Then the pilgrim stops counting the number of prayers; he unites the prayer "Lord Jesus Christ, Son of God, have mercy on me a sinner" with every breath, with every heart-beat. The moment comes when no word is pronounced any more: his

---

[1] [This seems in fact to be the third edition. According to A. Solignac, in *Dictionnaire de Spiritualité* 12 (1984), col. 886, a first edition, now impossible to find, appeared around 1870, and a second edition, revised by Theophan the Recluse, was published at Kazan in 1881.]

lips remain silent and all he has now to do is to listen to
the heart speaking. The Jesus Prayer serves him as food
when hungry, as drink when thirsty, as rest when weary, as
protection against wolves and other dangers. It inspires him
in the conversations that he has with those he meets,
common people like himself. Here are a few significant
passages:

"My whole desire was fixed on one thing alone, to say
the Jesus Prayer, and, as soon as I devoted myself to it, I
was filled with joy and consolation. It was as though my
lips and my tongue pronounced the words by themselves
without any effort on my part."

". . .Then I felt something like a slight burning sensation
in my heart and such a love for Jesus Christ in my thoughts
that I imagined that I was casting myself at his feet—if
only I could see him—and holding him in my embrace,
kissing his feet affectionately and thanking him with tears
for having allowed me, in his grace and his love, to find
such great consolation in his name—I, his unworthy and
sinful creature. Then there welled up within my heart a
pleasing warmth which spread throughout my breast. . ."

"Sometimes my heart would feel as if it were bursting
with joy, so light was it and full of freedom and consolation. Sometimes I would feel a burning love towards
Jesus Christ and all of God's creatures. . . .Sometimes, by
invoking the name of Jesus, I was overcome with happiness,
and from then on I knew the meaning of these words: *The
kingdom of God is within you.*"

Is *The Way of a Pilgrim* really an autobiography? Or is it
a spiritual novel, perhaps a piece of propaganda? In that
case, from what milieu did it emanate? We are obliged to
leave all of these questions unanswered. Everything in the
work is not fashioned from gold of the same purity. The
Jesus Prayer is presented in it a little too much as though it
were acting *ex opere operato.* A theologian, a monastic
superior, a priest in charge of souls would express himself
much more soberly and prudently. But one cannot be in-
sensible to the freshness of the narrative, to its evident

sincerity, often to its spiritual beauty, and finally to the literary gifts of the author.

The Way has a sequel. A second part, attributed to the same author as the first, appeared twenty-seven years later, under the same mysterious conditions.[2] This second part is rather different. It theologizes; it reproduces conversations in which, in one case, a professor and a *starets* intervene; it lacks the naïveté (perhaps only apparent) and the charm of the original work, and it seems unlikely that both were written by the same pen. We shall see later how the pilgrim has been received in the Western world of our own day.

*

*   *

The history of the Jesus Prayer in the first years of the 20th century includes a regrettable episode that took place at Mount Athos. The monk-priest Antony Bulatovich, a former officer in the Russian Army, and another monk, Hilarion, who had been a hermit in the Caucasus, propagated in Russian monastic circles on the Holy Mountain, about the year 1912, a doctrine according to which the actual name of Jesus is the Divinity. Those who upheld this doctrine were called "glorifiers of the name" *(imenoslavtsi* in Russian). Joachim III, Patriarch of Constantinople, condemned the doctrine as heretical; but the "glorifiers of the name" persisted in their teaching and greatly disturbed the peninsula. In 1913 the imperial Russian government sent a

---

[2]The sequel to *The Way of the Pilgrim* was published in 1911 at the Monastery of St Sergius in Moscow. No clear or satisfactory explanation of the origins of the work has been given. The continuation of the *Way* has been attributed to the famous *starets*, Ambrose of Optina (†1891). At least it seems an established fact that Fr Ambrose possessed a manuscript of the second part. That he was the author of it seems extremely doubtful. [On Fr Ambrose, see John B. Dunlop, *Staretz Amvrosy. Model for Dostoevsky's Staretz Zosima* (Belmont, Mass., 1972). In common with Fr Lev, Fr Ambrose recommended the repetition of the name "Jesus" entirely on its own (Dunlop, p. 159).]

steamship to Athos, even though it was within Greek ter-
ritory, and had the recalcitrant monks arrested by Russian
sailors. The "glorifiers of the name" were deported to
Russia. Echoes of this quarrel were still to be heard during
the First World War.[3]

The "glorifiers of the name" had expressed themselves
in a crude and clumsy way on a subject that requires the
utmost discernment. Their theory was obviously inadmis-
sible, but they had touched on a real problem. The late Fr
Sergius Bulgakov (1871-1944), of the Russian Institute of
Orthodox Theology in Paris, has posed this problem in
precise terms. Allow us to quote at some length from the
famous Russian theologian:

"The most important means for the life of the prayer is
the *Name of God* invoked in prayer. . . .What is most
important in prayer, what constitutes its very heart, is what
is called the Jesus Prayer: 'Lord Jesus Christ, Son of God,
have mercy on me a sinner.' This prayer, repeated hun-
dreds of times, or even continually, forms the essential
component of every rule of monastic prayer; it may even,
if need be, replace the Office and all other prayers, for its
value is universal. The power of this prayer does not reside
in its content, which is simple and clear—it is the prayer of
the tax-collector—but in the Most Sweet Name of Jesus.
The ascetics testify that this name has in it God's power
and presence. Not only is God invoked by this name, but
he is already present in the invocation.[4] This may of course
be said about every one of God's names; but it is especially
true of the divine-human name of Jesus which is his proper

---

[3]See *Collection of Documents concerning the Disturbances of the "Adorers of
the Name" on Athos* (in Russian) (Petrograd, 1916). [Cf. B. Schultze, "Der Streit um
die Göttlichkeit des Namens Jesu in der russischen Theologie," in *Orientalia
Christiana Periodica* 17 (1951), pp. 321-94; C.N. Papoulidis, Οἱ Ρῶσοι 'Ονοματο-
λάτραι τοῦ 'Αγίου 'Όρους (Thessalonica, 1977).]

[4]Needless to say, for Fr Bulgakov there cannot here be any question of God's
substantial presence in the divine name. He is referring rather to a dynamic
presence. The name is as it were an effective sign of the divine action, a kind of
sacrament (extending the meaning of this word beyond the use normal in theology
today).

name as both God and man. In short, the name of Jesus, present in the human heart, communicates to it the power of deification[5] which the Redeemer has granted to us. . . Shining through the heart, the light of the name of Jesus illumines the whole universe. This state cannot be described in words, but it is already a foreshadowing of the Last Day when 'God will be all in all'. . . .

"The practice of the Jesus Prayer has naturally led to theological discussions about the name of God and its power, about the meaning of the veneration of the name of God and about its active force. These questions have not yet received a solution having the force of dogma for the Church as a whole; indeed, they have not been sufficiently considered by theological literature. For the moment two different approaches exist. The first group, who call themselves 'glorifiers of God's name,' adopt a realist attitude towards the significance of the name in general. They believe that the name of God, invoked in prayer, already contains God's presence (Fr John of Kronstadt and others). The second group prefers a more rationalist and nominalist point of view: the name of God is regarded as a human, instrumental means for expressing the soul's thought about God and its striving towards him. Those who practice the Jesus Prayer, and mystics in general, uphold the first opinion, along with certain theologians and members of the hierarchy. The second point of view is characteristic of the school of Orthodox theology that reflects the influence of European rationalism.[6] In any event, the theological doctrine of the name of God is a problem of the present time, a problem essential to the expression and comprehension of

---

[5]"Deification" is understood here in the sense of the Greek Fathers: participation and union, but not identity of nature. Uncreated being and created being will always remain different as far as their essence is concerned. See M. Lot-Borodine, *La déification de l'homme selon la doctrine des Pères grecs* (Paris, 1970).

[6]Has Fr Bulgakov considered a third hypothesis? Between the "sacramental" and the "pedagogical" conception of the name, there is room for an intermediate conception: when the name of Jesus is formed *by the Holy Spirit* in our prayer and in our soul, it acquires, by the very fact of the Spirit's operation, and in so far as it results from it, a value *sui generis* in the order of grace. It is then a fruit of the Spirit.

Orthodoxy, a problem that our epoch bequeaths to future
generations. This problem indicates the principal path that
lies open before contemporary theological thinking."[7]

Fr S. Bulgakov also left a work, unpublished at the time
of his death, on *The Philosophy of the Name* (in Russian:
Paris, 1953). This deals with the name in general rather than
the name of God, but in the author's thought the whole
question was closely linked with the Jesus Prayer.[8]

*

*   *

It was while in the emigration that Fr Bulgakov wrote
the lines that we have quoted; indeed, it is within the
Russian emigration that a veritable renaissance of the Jesus
Prayer has taken place. This renaissance has been apparent
in the private devotions of the faithful rather than in the
official attitude of the Church. The *Dobrotolubie* has enjoyed a successful revival.[9] *The Way of the Pilgrim* has
been republished.[10] Moreover, it has been translated into
various Western languages, and this work so characteristic
of Orthodox Russia has been received with unexpected
favor by Romans, Anglicans, Lutherans and Calvinists. The
work has become, as they say, one of the "minor classics"

---

[7]*The Orthodox Church* (London, 1935), pp. 170-2 (English translation revised).

[8]L. Zander, in his article "Père Serge Boulgakov," in *Irénikon* 19 (1946), p. 181,
states that the first part of *The Philosophy of the Name* has been published in
German translation; unfortunately no precise reference to this translation is given.
The author of the article expresses himself thus: "This last book was envisaged [by
Fr Bulgakov] as a philosophical study of *onomatodoxy*, the mystical doctrine of the
veneration of God's name, based upon the traditions of Hesychasm and of St
Gregory Palamas."

[9]A new abridged edition appeared in Harbin in 1928; [a five-volume reissue of
Theophan's full text was published by the Russian Monastery of the Holy Trinity,
Jordanville, New York, in 1963-6.]

[10]The first part of the *Way* was re-edited in Russian by B. Vycheslavtsev in Paris,
1930. The second part was abridged and re-edited in Russian by Priest-monk (now
Archbishop) Seraphim in Ladimirova (Slovakia) in 1933. [Further editions of both
parts appeared in Russian at Paris in 1948 and 1973.]

of devotional literature.[11] The monks of the Russian monastery of Valamo in Finland have published two volumes of selected texts on the Jesus Prayer from Patristic and ascetic authors.[12]

*

* *

More than any other Western country, England has given close attention to the Jesus Prayer. Evelyn Underhill (pseudonym for Mrs. Stuart Moore, 1875-1941), one of Von Hügel's Anglican disciples, who has done so much to interest her country in mystical authors and in questions of the spiritual life, spoke of the Jesus Prayer in admirable

---

[11]The first French translation of the *Way of the Pilgrim* was published, without the translator's name, in *Irénikon-Collection*, 1928, nos. 5-7. A new French translation by J. Gauvain (pseudonym for J. Laloy), under the title *Récits d'un pèlerin russe*, was published in *Cahiers du Rhone* 12 (Neuchâtel, 1943); this was reprinted in the collection "Livre de Vie" (Paris, 1966). A German translation entitled *Ein russisches Pilgerleben*, by Rheinhold von Walter, preceded the French translations (Berlin, 1925). A Benedictine monk of Prinknash Abbey, Dom Theodore Baily, published in London, in 1930, an English version, *The Story of a Russian Pilgrim*, based on the French translation in *Irénikon*. Likewise in London and in 1930, the Rev. R.M. French published another translation, *The Way of the Pilgrim*. We do not know whether Baily's or French's translation can claim priority; curiously neither of these translations mentions the other. French does not state precisely on what Russian text his version was based and remains silent about previous continental translations. Hence the whole affair is cloaked in a certain mystery, the translations as well as the original. The translations that we have so far mentioned give only the first part of the *Way*. [The second part appeared in French translation under the title *Le Pèlerin russe. Trois récits inédits*, with an introduction by O. Clément (Bellefontaine, 1973).] R.M. French translated the second part into English as *The Pilgrim Continues his Way* (London, 1943). Both parts of French's translation were reissued in a single volume (London, 1954). [The two parts have since been reissued separately: *The Way of a Pilgrim*, with a new introduction by Metropolitan Anthony of Sourozh (London, 1972); *The Pilgrim Continues his Way* (London, 1973). More recently a new English translation has been made by Helen Bacovcin (Image Books, New York, 1978).]

[12]*The Mental Art. On the Jesus Prayer* (1936); *The Jesus Prayer in the Tradition of the Orthodox Church* (1938). [The first of these volumes has appeared in an English edition: Igumen Chariton, *The Art of Prayer: An Orthodox Anthology*, translated by E. Kadloubovsky and E.M. Palmer (London, 1966).]

terms: "This technique [is] so simple that it is within the
reach of the humblest worshipper, yet so penetrating that it
can introduce those who use it faithfully into the deepest
mysteries of the contemplative life. . .It carries the simple
and childlike appeal of the devout peasant, and the con-
tinuous self-acting aspiration of the great contemplative."[13]

It was through the Fellowship of St Alban and St Sergius,[13a] to which she belonged, that Evelyn Underhill came
into contact with Russian spirituality. The Fellowship is
entitled to a mention in a history of the Jesus Prayer because of the way in which its non-Orthodox members have
learned, through their contact with the Orthodox members,
what the Prayer is. It is a subject that has been treated
many times in lectures and retreats organized by the Fellowship. A number of English people have begun actually
to practice the Jesus Prayer. We were recently surprised to
meet an Englishman who, without having read anything on
the subject, devoted himself to it—and in a very serious
and fruitful way—because another Englishman had spoken
to him about it. The Dominicans of Oxford welcomed an
article in their monthly publication by an Orthodox writer
who speaks of the Jesus Prayer in such accurate terms that
we should like to quote part of it here:

"Many seem to have built their whole spiritual life on
the prayer of Jesus. . .A certain bodily technique was
practiced and recommended by the masters of the prayer:
immobility, regular breathing, fixing the eyes upon 'the
heart,' etc.. . .These 'physical' exercises were allowed only
to those who had an experienced director to help them. All
the Fathers emphasized, however, that such methods were
only 'crutches' to support the body and soul while one is
gaining control of oneself. The aim was to purify the body
and to make it an instrument of prayer. . .The invocation
was repeated vocally as well as mentally. . .To avoid me-

---

[13]*Worship* (London, 1936), p. 273.

[13a][An organization, founded in Britain in 1928, which aims at promoting closer
links between Orthodox and Western Christian (especially Anglicans). Fr Lev was
for many years chaplain to the Fellowship, residing at its permanent centre in
London, St. Basil's House.]

chanical repetition one modified words from time to time, but not too often. . .Some found it sufficient to call out: 'Jesu, Jesu'. . ."

"Is this a prayer for monks who alone can dedicate their whole time to it? The prayer of Jesus is in fact widely practiced by the lay people of the Orthodox Church. So simple is it that no learning is required for remembering it. It can rest on the lips of the sick too weak to say a *Pater* . . .Many go about their usual work repeating this prayer. Housework, ploughing, factory labor are not incompatible with it, and in fact the drudgery of some forms of manual work can be a help to concentration. It is possible, too, though more difficult, to join intellectual occupations with this continual prayer. It saves one from many uncharitable, vain words or thoughts: it sanctifies one's daily toil and relationships. The words become familiar; they seem after a time to flow of themselves. More and more they bring one into the *practice of the Presence of God* . . .Gradually, the words may seem to disappear; a *silent,* speechless *vigil* with a profound peace of heart and mind is sustained through the bustle of daily life. But in cases of distraction, temptation, tiredness or aridity it is useful to recur again to the vocal invocation: . . .'I sleep, but my heart waketh' (Song of Songs 5:2). The act of prayer has passed into a state of prayer."

"Like every spiritual way, this one needs fidelity, perseverance, courage. But this continual memory of Jesus Christ deepens in us and throws a new light on one's whole life. It becomes linked with the remembrance of Calvary and of the Last Supper; our communion and the sacrifice of the altar penetrate the heart, mind and will offered to the incessant invocation of the name of Jesus. On the other hand, we can apply this name to people, books, flowers, to all things we meet, see or think. The name of Jesus may become a mystical key to the world, an instrument of the hidden offering of everything and everyone, setting the divine seal on the world. One might perhaps speak here of the priesthood of all believers. In union with our High

Priest, we implore the Spirit: Make my prayer into a *sacrament.*"[14]

The principal interest of the article from which we have just quoted so extensively is that it constitutes a kind of synthesis of the *intentions* of the Jesus Prayer and its practical use. It opens up avenues and perspectives, showing what possibilities are offered for a loving and prayerful exploration of the name of Jesus. We notice particularly what is said of the eucharistic aspect of the Jesus Prayer: it can become in effect an offering and a communion. We notice also the suggestions about the *application* of the name of Jesus to persons and things in everyday life, and about the use of this name as a means towards the transfiguration of the world; we find here a very concrete development of the theology of the Body of Christ.

It is perhaps appropriate to add here a series of headings about the Jesus Prayer, which form part of an outline "Scheme of Studies" proposed by the Fellowship of St Alban and St Sergius to its members:

"The Name of Jesus and the 'Jesus Prayer.' The 'Jesus Prayer' as: (a) A call to meditation and intercession; (b) a realization of the Presence; (c) a sacrificial offering; (d) a sharing in the joy and strength of the Resurrection; (e) a coming of the Holy Spirit; (f) an instrument of transfiguration of men and things. Its technique and possibilities. Its link with the use of the Name of God in the Old Testament and with the Name of Jesus in the Acts of the Apostles."[15]

---

[14]"The Prayer of Jesus," in *Blackfriars* XXIII, no. 263 (February 1942), pp. 74-78. The author of the article , Mrs Nadejda Gorodetzky (1901-85), Professor of Russian at the University of Liverpool, also wrote *The Humiliated Christ in Modern Russian Thought* (London, 1938), and *St Tikhon Zadonsky, Inspirer of Dostoevsky* (Crestwood, 1976), two books that are of great help towards an understanding of Russian spirituality.

[15]See *Sobornost'*, New Series, no. 26 (December 1942), p. 22. Compare also E. Behr-Sigel, "La Prière à Jésus, ou le mystère de la spiritualité monastique orthodoxe," in *Dieu Vivant* 8 (1947), pp. 69-94; English translation, "Prayer to Jesus or the Essence of Orthodox monastic Spirituality," in *Eastern Churches Quarterly* 7 (1947), pp. 132-50. Cf. "A Monk of the Eastern Church" (Lev Gillet), *On the Invocation of the Name of Jesus* (Fellowship of St Alban and St Sergius, London,

For those who find congenial the horizons opened up in this "Scheme of Studies," the Jesus Prayer is not just a relic of the past. If we approach it with discretion and respect, it could bring new life to our souls. This renewal could serve the cause of Christian unity, for the invocation of the name of Jesus was at the very beginning common to all, and it still remains acceptable and accessible to all.[16] But its purpose is not only to re-establish bonds between those who find themselves divided, but first of all and above all to rekindle devotion to our Lord.

*

*   *

We have tried to give some idea of what the Jesus Prayer has been and still is. We hope that an historian will devote himself to this subject and write a book worthy of it. But any historical study on the Jesus Prayer, however exhaustive, will never be more than an introduction, leading the reader to the true point of departure, the point where facts and intellectual criticism are no longer enough, and where our will and love are also involved. If such a work is ever written, its most suitable conclusion will be the words with which St Bernard—one of the Latin Fathers who has spoken best about the name of Jesus—ends the five books that he addressed to Pope Eugenius III:

"We should seek him whom never yet have we sufficiently found, whom we can never seek too much; but perhaps it is through prayer rather than learned discussion that he is the more worthily sought and the more easily found. Let this, then, be the end of our work, but not the end of our search."[17]

1950; reprinted by SLG Press, Fairacres, Oxford, 1970); "L'Invocation du nom de Jésus dans la tradition byzantine," in *La Vie Spirituelle* (1952), pp. 38-45.

[16]Cf. Appendix II.

[17]End of *De Consideratione* (*PL* 182, cols. 807-8).

CHAPTER VI

ON THE PRACTICAL USE OF THE JESUS PRAYER

1. THE FORM OF THE PRAYER

The Byzantine East, as we have seen, has somewhat inadequately designated by the term "Jesus Prayer" every kind of invocation centering upon the actual name of the Savior. This invocation has assumed various specific forms according to whether the name was used alone or inserted into more or less developed formulas. It rests, however, with each individual to determine his or her own form of the invocation of the name. In the East the invocation became crystallized in the formula "Lord Jesus Christ, Son of God, have mercy on me a sinner," but this formula has never been and is not the only one. Every *repeated* invocation, in which the name of Jesus forms the core and motive force, is authentically the "Jesus Prayer" in the Byzantine sense. One may say, for example, "Jesus Christ" or "Lord Jesus." The oldest, the simplest, and in our opinion the easiest formula is the word "Jesus" used alone. It is with this last possibility in mind that we shall speak here of the "Jesus Prayer."

This type of prayer may be pronounced or merely thought. Its place is thus on the boundary between vocal and mental prayer, between prayer of meditation and prayer of contemplation. It may be practiced at all times and in any place: church, bedroom, street, office, workshop, and so on. We can repeat the name while walking. Beginners, however, will do well to bind themselves to a certain regularity in their practice of the Prayer, choosing fixed times and solitary places. Yet this systematic training does not exclude a parallel and entirely free use of the invocation of the name.

Before beginning to pronounce the name of Jesus, we should try first of all to put ourselves in a state of peace and recollection, and then implore the help of the Holy Spirit in whom alone we can "say that Jesus is the Lord" (1 Cor 12:3). Every other preliminary is superfluous. In order to swim one must first throw oneself into the water; similarly we must in one leap cast ourselves into the name of Jesus. Having begun to pronounce the name with loving adoration, all that we have to do is to attach ourselves to it, cling to it, and to repeat it slowly, gently and quietly. It would be a mistake to "force" this prayer, to raise our voice inwardly, to try to induce intensity and emotion. When God manifested himself to the prophet Elijah, it was not in a strong wind, nor in an earthquake, nor in a fire, but in the gentle, whispering breeze that followed them (1 Kgs 19:11-12). Little by little we are to concentrate our whole being around the name, allowing it like a drop of oil silently to penetrate and impregnate our soul. When invoking the name, it is not necessary to repeat it continually. Once spoken, the name then may be "prolonged" for several minutes of repose, of silence, of purely interior attention, much as a bird alternates between the flapping of its wings and gliding flight.

All tension and haste are to be avoided. If fatigue comes upon us, the invocation should be interrupted and taken up again simply when one feels drawn towards it. Our aim is not a constant, literal repetition but a kind of latent and quiescent presence of the name of Jesus in our heart. "I sleep, but my heart keeps vigil" (Song of Songs 5:2). Let us banish all spiritual sensuality, all pursuit of emotion. No doubt it is natural to hope to obtain results that are in some measure tangible, to want to touch the hem of the Savior's garment and not to give up until he has blessed us (cf. Mt 9:21; Gn 32:26). But let us not think that an hour during which we have invoked the name without "feeling" anything, remaining apparently cold and arid, has been wasted and unfruitful. This invocation that we thought sterile will be, on the contrary, highly acceptable to God, since it is chemically pure, if we may put it that way, because stripped of all preoccupation with spiritual delights and reduced to an offering of the naked will. At other times in his generous mercy the Savior often enfolds his name in an atmosphere of joy, warmth and light: "Thy name is as oil poured forth. . .draw me" (Song of Songs 1:3-4)

2. EPISODE OR METHOD?

For some the invocation of the name will be an episode on their spiritual journey; for others it will be more than an episode, it will be one of the methods they habitually use, yet without being *the* method; for yet others it will be *the* method around which their whole interior life is organized. To decide by arbitrary choice, by some whim, that this last case will be ours, would be like constructing a building which then collapses wretchedly. We do not choose the "Jesus Prayer." We are called to it, led to it by God, if he thinks it right. We devote ourselves to it out of obedience to a very special vocation, provided that other obediences do not have prior right. If this form of prayer does not stand in the way of the other forms to which we are committed by virtue of our state in life, if it is accompanied by a pressing attraction, if it produces in us fruits of purity, charity and peace, if our appointed spiritual guides encourage us to practice it, there is in all this, if not the infallible signs of a vocation, then at least indications which deserve to be humbly and attentively considered.

The "way of the name" has been approved by many Eastern monastic Fathers and also by several saints of the West. It is therefore legitimate and remains open as a possibility for all. But we should avoid all indiscreet zeal, all untimely propaganda. We should not cry out with an ill-informed fervor, "It is the best prayer," much less, "It is the only prayer." We should keep hidden in their secret place the mysteries of the King. Those who are bound to a community or to a rule will discern to what extent the way of the name is compatible with the methods to which they

owe obedience; the appropriate authorities will help them
in this task of discernment. We are not referring here to
liturgical prayer; for this could not enter into conflict with
the kind of inner prayer that we are discussing. In particular we would not wish to suggest to those whose existing
prayer is an authentic dialogue with the Lord, nor to those
who are established in the deep silence of the contemplative life, that they should abandon their way of prayer
in order to practice the "Jesus Prayer." We do not de-
preciate the value of any form of prayer. For in the final
analysis the best prayer for each person is the one, which-
ever it may be, to which each is drawn by the Holy Spirit,
by particular circumstances, and by properly appointed
spiritual direction.

What we may say with soberness and truth on behalf of
the "Jesus Prayer" is that it helps to simplify and unify
our spiritual life. When complicated methods dissipate and
weary the attention, this "one-word prayer" possesses the
power of unification and integration, assisting the frag-
mented soul that finds its name and its sin to be "legion"
(Mk 5:9). The name of Jesus, once it has become the
center of our life, brings everything together. But let us not
imagine that the invocation of the name is a "short-cut" that
dispenses us from ascetic purification. The name of Jesus is
itself an instrument of asceticism, a filter through which
should pass only thoughts, words and acts compatible with
the divine and living reality which this name symbolizes.
The growth of the name in our soul implies a correspond-
ing diminution of our separated self, a daily death to the
selfcentredness from which all sin is derived.

3.   THE FIRST STEPS. ADORATION AND SALVATION

There are many levels in the "Jesus Prayer." It grows
deeper and broader as we discover each new level in the
name. It should begin as adoration and a sense of presence.
Then, this presence is experienced specifically as that of a
Savior (for such is the meaning of the word "Jesus"). The

invocation of the name is a mystery of salvation in the sense that it brings with it deliverance. In uttering the name, we already receive what we need. We receive it here and now in Jesus who is not only the giver but the gift; not only the purifier, but all purity; not only the one who feeds the hungry and gives drink to the thirsty, but who is himself our food and drink. He is the substance of. all good things (if we do not use this term in a strictly metaphysical sense).

His name gives peace to those who are tempted: instead of arguing with the temptation, instead of thinking about the raging storm—that was Peter's mistake on the lake after his good beginning—why not look at Jesus alone and go to him walking on the waves, taking refuge in his name? Let the person tempted gather himself together gently and pronounce the name without anxiety, without feverishness; then his heart will be filled by the name and in this way protected against violent winds. If a sin has been committed, let the name serve as a means of immediate reconciliation. Without hesitation or delay, let it be pronounced with repentance and perfect charity, and it will become at once a token of pardon. In an altogether natural way Jesus will take his place again in the life of the sinner, just as after his Resurrection he came back and sat in such a simple manner at table with the disciples who had deserted him, and then offered him fish and honey (Lk 24:41-42). Of course we do not intend to reject or underestimate the objective means of repentance and absolution which the Church offers to the sinner; we are speaking here only of what happens in the hidden places of the soul.

4.   INCARNATION

The name of Jesus is more than a mystery of salvation, more than help in time of need, more than pardon after sin. It is a means by which we can apply to ourselves the mystery of the Incarnation. Beyond his presence, it brings union. By pronouncing the name, we enthrone Jesus in our

hearts, we put on Christ; we offer our flesh to the Word so
that he may assume it into his Mystical Body; we cause the
interior reality and the power of the word "Jesus" to over-
flow into our members that are subject to the law of sin.
In this way we are purified and consecrated. "Set me as a
seal upon thy heart, as a seal upon thy arm" (Song of
Songs 8:6). But the invocation of the name of Jesus does
more than enable us to appreciate the meaning of the
mystery of the Incarnation for ourselves personally. Through
this prayer we also catch a glimpse of the "fullness of him
who fills all in all" (Eph. 1:23).

5. TRANSFIGURATION

The name of Jesus is an instrument and method of
transfiguration. When we utter it, it helps us to transfigure
—without any pantheistic confusion—the whole world into
Jesus Christ.

This is true even of inanimate nature. The material
universe, which is not only the visible symbol of the invisible divine beauty, but which turns with "groaning"
toward Christ (Rom 8:22), and whose mysterious movement elevates all that comes into being towards the Bread
and Wine of salvation, this universe murmurs secretly the
name of Jesus: ". . .even the stones will cry out. . ." (Lk
19:40). It belongs to the priestly ministry of each Christian
to give a voice to this aspiration, to pronounce the name of
Jesus upon the elements of nature, stones and trees, flowers
and fruit, mountains and sea, and so to bring to fulfillment
the secret of things, to provide an answer to that long,
silent and unconscious expectation.

We can also transfigure the animal world. Jesus, who
declared that not a sparrow is forgotten by his Father
(Lk 12:6) and who dwelt in the desert "with the wild
beasts" (Mk 1:13), did not leave the beasts outside the
sphere of his goodness and influence. Like Adam in Paradise we are to give a name to all the animals. Whatever the
name that science gives to them, we shall invoke upon each

one of them the name of Jesus, thereby giving back to them their primitive dignity which we so often forget, and remembering that they are created and loved by the Father in Jesus and for Jesus.

But it is especially in relation to our fellow humans that the name of Jesus helps us to exercise a ministry of transfiguration. Jesus, who after his Resurrection chose several times to appear to his disciples "in another form" (Mk 16:12)—the unknown traveller on the road to Emmaus, the gardener near the tomb, the stranger standing on the shore of the lake—continues to meet us in our daily life in a veiled way and to confront us with this all-important aspect of his presence: his presence in man. What we do to the least of our brethren, we do to him. Under the faces of men and women we are able, with our eyes of faith and love, to see the face of the Lord; by attending to the distress of the poor, of the sick, of sinners, of all men, we put our finger on the place of the nails, thrust our hands into his pierced side, and experience personally the Resurrection and the real presence (without any confusion of essence) of Jesus Christ in his Mystical Body; and so we can say with St Thomas, "My Lord and my God" (Jn 20:28).

The name of Jesus is a concrete and powerful means of transfiguring men into their most profound and divine reality. Let us reach out toward the men and women whom we pass in the street, the factory or the office — and especially toward those who seem to us irritating or antipathetic — with the name of Jesus in our heart and on our lips. Let us pronounce silently over them his name, which is their very own name; let us call them by this name in a spirit of adoration and service. Let us devote ourselves to them in a practical way, if that is possible, or at all events by an interior aspiration, for in them we are really devoting ourselves to Jesus Christ. By recognizing and silently adoring Jesus imprisoned in the sinner, in the criminal, in the prostitute, we release in some way both these poor jailers and our Master. If we see Jesus in everyone, if we say "Jesus" over everyone, we will go through the world with a new vision and a new gift in our own heart.

In this way, as far as lies in our power, we can transform
the world and make our own the words that Jacob spoke
to his brother: "I have seen thy face, and it is as though I
had seen the face of God" (Gn 33:10).

6. THE BODY OF CHRIST

The invocation of the name of Jesus has an ecclesial
aspect. In this name we meet all those who are united with
the Lord and in the midst of whom he stands. In this name
we can embrace all those who are enclosed within the
Divine Heart. To intercede for another is not so much to
plead on his behalf before God, but rather to apply to his
name the name of Jesus and to unite ourselves to the intercession of our Lord himself for his loved ones.

Here we touch upon the mystery of the Church. Where
Jesus Christ is, there is the Church. The name of Jesus is a
means of uniting us to the Church, for the Church is in
Christ. In him the Church is unsullied. It is not that we seek
to dissociate ourselves from the existence and the problems
of the Church on earth, or to close our eyes to the imper-
fections and disunity of Christians. We do not wish to
separate or oppose the visible and invisible aspects of the
Church. But we know that what is implied in the name of
Jesus is the spotless, spiritual and eternal aspect of the
Church which transcends every earthly manifestation and
which no schism can destroy. When Jesus speaks to the
Samaritan woman about the hour that "comes and now is"
(Jn 4:23) in which the true worshipers will worship the
Father, no longer in Jerusalem or on Garizim, but in spirit
and truth, there is an apparent contradiction in his words.
How can the hour already have come and yet still be
coming? The paradox is explained by the fact that the
Samaritan woman was standing at that moment before Jesus.
Certainly the opposition between Jerusalem and Garizim still
existed, and Jesus, far from minimizing it, had declared that
salvation comes from the Jews: therefore the hour was still
to come. But, because Jesus was there and in his person

Jerusalem and Garizim are infinitely transcended, the hour had already come. When we invoke the name of the Savior we are in an analogous situation. We cannot believe that divergent interpretations of the Gospel are all equally true or that divided Christians all possess the same measure of light; but we do believe that those who, in pronouncing the name of Jesus, try to unite themselves to their Lord by an act of unconditional obedience and perfect charity, transcend human divisions, participate in some way in the supernatural unity of the Mystical Body of Christ and are, if not visible and explicit, at least invisible and implicit members of the Church. And thus the invocation of the name of Jesus, made with an upright heart, is a way towards Christian unity.

It also helps us meet again, in Jesus, the faithful departed. To Martha who professed her faith in the future Resurrection, Jesus replied: "I *am* the Resurrection and the Life" (Jn 11:25). This means that the resurrection of the dead is not merely a future event; that the person of the risen Christ is already the resurrection and the life of all the redeemed; and that instead of seeking, either through prayer or by the memory and the imagination, to establish a direct spiritual contact between our departed and ourselves, we should try to reach them in Jesus, where their true life now is, linking the name of Jesus to their own names. These departed, whose life is hidden in Christ, are within the heavenly Church that forms the most numerous part of the eternal and total Church.

In the name of Jesus we meet the saints who bear "his name on their foreheads" (Rev 22:4), and also the angels, one of whom said to Mary, "Thou shalt call his name Jesus" (Lk 1:31), as well as Mary herself. Let us in the Spirit seek to hear and to repeat the name of Jesus as Mary heard it and repeated it!

7.   THE SUPPER OF THE LORD

The name of Jesus can become for us a kind of Eu-

charist. Just as the mystery of the Upper Room was a
summing up of the Lord's whole life and mission, so also a
certain "eucharistic" use of the name of Jesus brings together
and unites all the aspects of the name considered thus far.

The sacramental Eucharist does not fall within the limits
of our theme. But our soul is also an upper room where
Jesus desires to eat the Passover with his disciples, and
where the Lord's Supper can be celebrated at any moment
whatever in an invisible way. In this purely spiritual Last
Supper, the name of the Savior can take place of the bread
and wine of the sacrament. We can make of the name of
Jesus an offering of thanksgiving—and this is the original
meaning of the word "eucharist"—the support and substance
of a sacrifice of praise rendered to the Father. In this
interior and invisible offering, we present to the Father, by
pronouncing the name of Jesus, a lamb sacrificed, a life
given, a body broken, blood poured out. The sacred name,
when used in this sacrificial way, becomes a means of
applying to ourselves here and now the fruits of the perfect
oblation offered once for all on Golgotha.

There is no Lord's Supper without communion. Our
invisible Eucharist implies what tradition has called "spiritual
communion," that is, the act of faith and desire by which
the soul is nourished on the Body and Blood of Christ
without making use of the visible elements of bread and
wine. Nothing could be further from our mind than to
diminish or underestimate the sacrament of the Eucharist, as
practiced by the Church, which we cannot simply identify
with spiritual communion. But we believe that we are
within the Church's authentic tradition in affirming the reality
of a constant, invisible, purely spiritual approach to the
Body and Blood of Christ, an approach which is distinct
from the general drawing-near to his person, for it implies a
special kind of relation between ourselves and the Savior,
who is considered in this instance as both the feeder and the
food of our souls. The name of Jesus can be used as the
form, support and expression of this approach. It can be for
us a spiritual food, a sharing in the Bread of Life. "Lord,
give us always of this bread" (Jn 6:34). In his name, in this

bread we are united to all the members of the Mystical Body of Christ, to all those who sit down at the banquet of the Messiah, we who "being many, are one bread, one body" (1 Cor 10:17).

And since the Eucharist proclaims "the death of the Lord, until he come" (1 Cor 11:26), since it is an anticipation of the eternal kingdom, the "eucharistic" use of the name of Jesus also possesses an "eschatological" meaning. It proclaims the "end" and the Second Coming, it is an ardent yearning, not only for the occasional "breakings-in" of Christ into our earthly life, but for that definitive coming of Christ to us which will be the moment of our death. There is a certain way of saying the name of Jesus which constitutes a preparation for death, a leaping of our heart beyond the barrier, a last general appeal to the Bridegroom "whom, without having seen, you love" (1 Pt 1:8). To say "Jesus" is therefore to repeat the cry of the Apocalypse: "Come, Lord Jesus" (Rev 22:20).

8. THE NAME AND THE SPIRIT

When we read the Acts of the Apostles, we see what a central place the name of Jesus occupied in the message and action of the apostles. Through them "the name of the Lord Jesus was magnified" (Acts 19:17); in this name miraculous signs were performed and lives were changed. After Pentecost the apostles became capable of proclaiming the name "with power." Here we have a "pentecostal" use of the name of Jesus, a use which is not the monopoly of the apostles, but which remains open to all believers. Only the weakness of our faith and charity prevents us from renewing in the name of Jesus the fruits of Pentecost, from driving out devils, from laying hands on the sick and curing them. Saints continue to act in this way. The Spirit writes the name of Jesus in fiery letters upon the hearts of his elect. This name is a burning flame within them.

But there also exists, between the Holy Spirit and the invocation of the name of Jesus, another link more interior

than the "pentecostal" ministry of the Christian. By pronouncing the name of our Savior, we can obtain a certain
"experience"—this word being used with all the necessary
reservations—of the relation between the Son and the Spirit.
We can make ourselves coincide with the descent of the
dove upon our Lord; we can unite our heart—in so far as a
creature can unite itself to a divine activity—to the eternal
movement of the Spirit towards Jesus. "Oh that I had wings
like a dove" (Ps 55:6), not only to take flight far from
earthly cares but to alight upon him who is all my good! O
if only I knew how to hear the "voice of the turtledove"
(Song of Songs 2:12), as she speaks with "sighs too deep for
words" (Rom 8:26) the name of the Beloved! Then the
invocation of the name of Jesus would be an initiation into
the mystery of the relationship of love between Christ and
the Spirit.

Conversely, we may strive to coincide—always respect-
ing the proper limits—with the reverse relationship, Jesus'
attitude towards the Holy Spirit. Conceived by the Spirit,
led by the Spirit, Jesus showed the most humble docility
towards the Breath of the Father. While pronouncing the
name of Jesus let us unite ourselves, in so far as this is
given to humans, to the complete surrender that Jesus
made of his life to this divine Breath.

Let us also see in the name of Jesus a hearth whence
the Spirit radiates, let us see in Jesus the point of departure
whence the Spirit is sent to men, the mouth whence the
Spirit is breathed upon us. The invocation of the name of
Jesus, uniting us with these various moments—Jesus being
filled by the Spirit, the sending of the Spirit to men by
Jesus, and also Jesus' yearning for the Father—will make us
grow in knowledge of, and union with, the one whom Paul
calls "the Spirit of his Son" (Gal 4:6).

9.   TOWARDS THE FATHER

There is the Son. And there is the Father. Our reading of
the Gospel will remain superficial as long as we see in it only

a life and a message directed to men. The heart of the Gospel, the mystery of Jesus, is the relationship between the Father and the only-begotten Son.

To utter the name of Jesus is to utter the Word which "was in the beginning" (Jn 1:1), the Word which the Father utters from all eternity. The name of Jesus, we might even say with a certain anthropomorphism (easily corrected), is the only human word which the Father utters as he begets the Son and gives himself to him. To utter the name of Jesus is to draw near the Father, to contemplate the love and the gift of the Father which is concentrated upon Jesus; it is to feel, to a limited extent, something of that love and to unite ourselves to it from afar; it is to hear the Father's voice declaring, "Thou art my beloved Son" (Lk 3:22), and humbly to respond "yes" to this declaration.

To utter the name of Jesus is, on the other hand, to enter, as much as a creature is able, into Christ's filial consciousness. After finding in the word "Jesus" the Father's tender appeal "My Son!", it is also to find in it the Son's tender response, "My Father!" It is to recognize in Jesus the perfect expression of the Father, to unite ourselves to the eternal orientation of the Son towards the Father, to the total offering of the Son to his Father. To utter the name of Jesus—if it is permissible to speak in this way—is in a certain fashion to join the Son to the Father and to glimpse some reflection of the mystery of their unity. It is to find the best approach to the Father's heart.

10.   JESUS IN HIS TOTALITY

We have considered various aspects of the invocation of the name of Jesus. We have arranged them in a kind of ascending ladder, perhaps pedagogically useful, but artificial, because in point of fact the various steps intermingle and "God does not give the Spirit by measure" (Jn 3:34). At various stages in the practice of the invocation of the name of Jesus, it can be good, even necessary, to concentrate our attention upon one or other particular aspect of

the divine name. But a moment comes when such speciali-
zation grows wearisome, difficult, and sometimes even
impossible. The contemplation and invocation of the name
of Jesus then becomes all-embracing. Every implication of
the name becomes simultaneously, although obscurely,
present to our mind. We say "Jesus," and we rest in a
plentitude and totality that can no longer be taken from us.
The name of Jesus then becomes a bearer of the whole
Christ. It brings us into his total presence.

In this total presence are found all the realities towards
which the name has served as a means of approach: salvation and pardon, the Incarnation and the Transfiguration,
the Church and the Eucharist, the Spirit and the Father.
All things then appear to us "gathered together in Christ"
(Eph 1:10). The total presence is all. The name is nothing
without the Presence. He who has attained the Presence has
no longer any need of the name. The name is only the
support of the Presence. At the end of the road, we are to
become free from the actual name, free from everything
except from Jesus, from the living and ineffable contact
with his person.

A ray of light brings together the various colors which
the prism scatters. Thus the "total name," the sign and
bearer of the total Presence, acts as a lens which receives
and concentrates the white light of Jesus. This lens helps us
to light the fire of which it was said: "I am come to cast
fire on the earth" (Lk 12:49). If we cling to the name of
Jesus, we shall receive the special blessing that Scripture
promises, "Have mercy on me as is thy custom toward
them that love thy name" (Ps 119:132). And may the Lord
be pleased to say of us what he said of Saul: "He is a
chosen vessel of mine, to bear my name" (Acts 9:15).

THE PSYCHO-PHYSIOLOGICAL METHOD
OF THE JESUS PRAYER

We are not bound to defend this method, but we should like to some extent to explain it. The slowing down or the retention of one's breathing is a well-known means of putting oneself in a state of calm. A man of such interior and deep spirituality as Vladimir Soloviev recommended this practice. St Ignatius Loyola in his *Exercises* advises "rhythmic prayer," "from one breath to another."[1] Each respiratory movement can emit a prayer. Furthermore, the Hesychasts attached great importance to maintaining the spirit "within the limits of the body;" we are, that is to say, to prevent the spirit from being dispersed in external things, which happens through the exercise of the visual, tactile and locomotive functions. If one retains one's breathing, if at the same time one remains motionless, with the eyes closed or lowered, and if this bodily attitude is accompanied by a psychological effort to "bring back the spirit into the body" and *not to go beyond the body's limits,* this operation, almost impossible to describe, produces a sense of constraint (which can become painful), but also a sense

---

[1][See the "Third Method of Prayer," in *The Text of the Spiritual Exercises of Saint Ignatius* (5th ed., London, 1952), pp. 89-90. Fr Hausherr discusses this comparison in his article, "Les Exercises Spirituels de Saint Ignace et la méthode d'oraison hésychaste," in *Orientalia Christiana Periodica* 20 (1954), pp. 7-26; reprinted in *Hésychasme et prière,* pp. 134-53. Fr Lev, it should be noted, does not claim that there is an exact parallel between Ignatius and the Hesychasts, but merely notes how in his teaching on prayer Ignatius takes advantage of the physical rhythm of respiration.]

of the sharply-defined concurrence between the spirit and the body, a sense of intense concentration.

As for "omphaloscopy" or fixation of the gaze upon the navel, neither the name nor the thing corresponds to what Hesychasm recommends. It has never been a question of contemplating the navel, which would be pure Yoga. It is a question of fixing the gaze, while in a seated position, on the middle of the body. The navel represents, in a somewhat naive fashion, a point of centering, an axis of direction; but it can be said with equal accuracy that the gaze is to be directed upon the chest.

"A bizarre practice, almost scandalous," writes Fr Jugie in his article on Gregory Palamas from which we have already quoted. For all that, we must try to understand it. The aim is to "find the place of the heart," to make the spirit descend into the heart. Disregarding an outdated physiology, this means that we are, while concentrating our gaze in the direction of the heart, vividly to picture our heart as the symbolic place of affective and volitional life, of love; then we are to cast into this blazing fire our "intellectual" thoughts and to allow them to become inflamed, to light up and catch fire through contact with this flame, until a burning cry breaks out within us and rises up toward Jesus.

This physical attitude, with the head bent towards the heart, is at the same time related to what Dionysius the Pseudo-Areopagite calls the "circular movement" of the soul. "The soul's movement is circular," he writes, "when, entering into itself, it turns away from things outside, and gathers into unity its spiritual powers" (On the Divine Names IV, 9; PG 3, col. 705A). This cyclic movement of prayer expresses the overflowing of the spirit within the heart, the circumincession or mutual penetration between the intellect and love. It also represents, albeit in a somewhat crude fashion, the circumincession of the Trinity, the communion of love between the Three Persons. Andrei Rublev's famous icon of the Trinity, which is perhaps the highest artistic expression of Orthodoxy, clearly suggests, even in its smallest details, a circular movement (which is counterclockwise).[2] In short, it is our aim, by means of bodily attitudes, to create powerful mental representations which in their turn release certain psychic dynamisms. The close relationship between mental representation and spatial arrangements has been stressed by the modern *Gestalt-Psychologie*.

Concerning the luminous vision to which the Jesus Prayer leads, let us distinguish four possibilities. There is in the first place the perception, by the natural organs, of a light produced supernaturally; this has happened to both saints and sinners. Next, far above the first, as a limiting case, there is the supernatural perception of a supernatural light, a perception that is not sensible or physical, and that consequently transcends normal psychology; this happens when the light of the Transfiguration is seen, not by the organs of sense-perception in their normal state, but by eyes already transfigured. At the bottom of the ladder, there is the purely symbolic use of the word "light," when name of Jesus is regarded in a figurative sense as the sun of the soul. Between this case and the one first considered, there is room for an intermediate possibility: the constant or frequent practice of the Jesus Prayer can place the one who prays in an habitual inner state of "luminosity." Even if he closes his eyes, he has the impression of being penetrated by radiance and of moving in light. This is more than a symbol; it is less than a sensible perception, and is certainly not an ecstasy; but it is something real, although indescribable.

We shall not enter into the "Palamite" question concerning the relationship between God's essence and the divine light. Let us remember only that oriental mysticism has always been a mysticism of light (as is already the case with the Jews and the Shekina or "glory"). "God is light."

---

[2][See Fr Lev's article, "La signification spirituelle de l'icône de la Sainte Trinité peinte par André Rublev," in *Contacts* XXXIII, 116 (1981), pp. 351-7; cf. *Irénikon* 26 (1953), pp. 133-40.]

APPENDIX II

THE INVOCATION OF THE NAME OF JESUS IN THE WEST

The Roman Church includes among its feasts that of the Holy Name of Jesus (which the Orthodox Church does not have); since Pius X this feast has been celebrated on the Sunday which falls between 1 January and Epiphany or, failing this, on 2 January.[1] The Mass and Office of the feast were composed by Bernardino dei Busti (†1500) and approved by Pope Sixtus IV. Originally confined to Franciscan houses, the feast was later extended to the whole Church. The style of the prayers bears the stamp of the period in which they were composed, and differs greatly from the old Roman style. One cannot but admire, however, the beauty of the Scripture lessons and of the Homilies of St Bernard chosen for Matins.

The hymns *Jesu dulcis memoria* and *Jesu rex admirabilis*, falsely attributed to St Bernard, are taken from a *jubilus* written by an unknown author of the 12th century. The litanies of the Holy Name of Jesus approved by Sixtus V are of doubtful origin; perhaps they were composed towards the beginning of the 15th century by St Bernardino of Siena and St John of Capistrano. These litanies, as the invocations indicate – "Jesus, splendor of the Father. . . Jesus, sun of righteousness. . .Jesus, meek and humble of heart. . .Jesus, lover of chasity. . ."– are devoted to the attributes rather than to the actual name of Jesus. One could to some extent compare them with the *akathist* of

---

[1][This observance was discontinued in the Roman Calendar of 1969. In many parts of the Anglican communion, following the late medieval practice in England the feast is kept on 7 August.]

111

the "Most Sweet Jesus" in the Byzantine Church.[2]

We know with what devotion the monogram IHS has been surrounded. It does not signify, as is often said, *Jesus Hominum Salvator*, but simply represents an abbreviation of the name of Jesus. The Jesuits, topping the H with a cross, have made this monogram the emblem of their Society. In 1564 Pope Pius IV approved a Confraternity of the Most Holy Names of God and Jesus, which later became the Society of the Holy Name of Jesus. It still exists. This foundation was a result of the Council of Lyons (1274) which prescribed a special devotion toward the name of Jesus. Fifteenth-century England used a *Jesus Psalter* composed by Richard Whytford; this comprises a series of petitions, each one of which begins with the triple mention of the sacred name. It is still in use and we have a very recent copy of it before us.

The great promoter of devotion to the name of Jesus during the later Middle Ages was St Bernardino of Siena (1380-1444). He recommended the carrying of tablets on which were inscribed the sign IHS and, by substituting these tablets for the Guelf and Ghibelline *graffitti* that covered the walls in the streets, he hoped to bring about a sense of peace in men's hearts (P. Thureau-Dangin, *Saint Bernardin de Sienne*, Paris, 1896). This propaganda earned him an attack from the Augustinian Andrew Biglia, in a long dissertation in two books, written in a restrained tone (see "Le memoire de'André Biglia sur la prédication de saint Bernardin de Sienne," text with introduction and notes by Fr B. de Gaiffier, in *Analecta Bollandiana* 53 [1935], pp. 307-365); and another attack, also from an Augustinian, Andrew de Cascia, in a more violent treatise addressed to Pope Martin V, in which we read: "This cult destroys faith in the Holy Trinity, it lowers the dignity of Christ's humanity; it sets aside the cult of the cross." Nevertheless Martin V and Eugenius IV declared Bernardino to be in the right. But the humanist Poggio denounced what he called *illa jesuitas* and

---

[2][Cf. S. Salaville, "Un Office grec du 'Très Doux Jésus' antérieur au 'Jubilus' dit de Saint Bernard," in *Revue d'Ascétique et de Mystique* 25 (1949), pp. 246-59.]

the "impudence of these men who, devoted to the name of Jesus alone, stir up a new heresy." St John of Capistrano, a disciple of Bernardino, was also a fervent promoter of devotion to the name of Jesus. The two saints belonged to the religious family of St Francis of Assisi. We know that Francis himself had a tender love for the name of Jesus. The cult of the Holy Name became a Franciscan tradition, and it is significant that an Italian version of the *Fioretti*, made at Trevi in 1458 by a Friar Minor of the Bernardine reform, contains an additional chapter on the cult rendered by St Francis to the name of Jesus (E. Landry, "Contribution à l'étude critique des Fioretti de saint Francois d' Assisi," in *Annales de la Faculté des Lettres de Bordeaux et des Universités du Midi*, 4th series, vol. 1 [1901], pp. 138-145).

But it is in the end St Bernard of Clairvaux, during the 12th century, who was the most inspired by the name of Jesus. One should read above all his fifteenth sermon on the Songs of Songs (*PL* 183, cols 843-7). Commenting on the verse of the Song comparing the name of Jesus to ointment that has been poured out (1:3), he develops the idea that the sacred name gives light, nourishes and anoints, exactly as oil does. "Is it not through the light of this name that God has called us to his wonderful light?" (One recalls the Hesychasts.) "The name of Jesus is not only light but also food." This name *castas fovet affectiones*, "cherishes chaste affections"—words that illumine with marvelous clarity the relationship between the Jesus Prayer and human friendship or conjugal love. Finally: "Write what you will, I shall take no pleasure in it unless I read there the name of Jesus. Talk or argue as you wish, I shall find it flat and dull unless I hear the name of Jesus. Jesus is honey in the mouth, melody in the ear, a sense of joy in the heart. But the name is also a remedy. Is any among you sad? Let Jesus come into his heart and from there spring up into his mouth. . .Does any fall into sin?. . .If he invokes the very name of life, will he not breathe at once the air of life?" These passages contain a most profound theology of the sacred name.

On the Latin cult of the name of Jesus, see in general
C. Stengel, *Sacrosancti nominis Jesu cultus et miracula*
(Augsburg, 1613); *Acta Sanctorum* (Brussels, 1861), October,
vol. 10, pp. 319-20.

FURTHER READING

History of the Jesus Prayer

The basic work, despite certain shortcomings, is still the scholarly study by Irénée Hausherr, SJ, *Noms du Christ et voies d'oraison* (*Orientalia Christiana Analecta* 157: Rome, 1960); English translation by Charles Cummings, OCSO, *The Name of Jesus* (*Cistercian Studies Series* 44: Kalamazoo, 1978). For a brief, clear summary of the main evidence, see Pierre Adnès, "Jésus (Prière à)," in *Dictionnaire de Spiritualité* 8 (1974), cols 1126-50. A short outline is also given by Kallistos Ware, "Ways of Prayer and Contemplation: I. Eastern," in Bernard McGinn and John Meyendorff (ed.), *Christian Spirituality: Origins to the Twelfth Century* (*World Spirituality: An Encyclopedic History of the Religious Quest*, vol. 16: New York, 1985), pp. 395-414. Important material in the Coptic sources, not mentioned by Gillet or Hausherr, is presented by André Guillaumont, "The Jesus Prayer among the Monks of Egypt," in *Eastern Churches Review* 6 (1974), pp. 66-71.

Sources: (i) Greek

The primary sources in Greek on the Jesus Prayer are to be found chiefly in the *Philokalia* of St Macarius of Corinth and St Nicodemus of the Holy Mountain. A full English version of this has begun to appear, translated from the original Greek by G.E.H. Palmer, Philip Sherrard and Kallistos Ware, *The Philokalia: The Complete Text*, with three volumes so far issued out of a total of five (London, 1979-84). For the 13th- and 14th-century texts, to be included in the two volumes, the English reader must for the time being continue to use the older translation by E. Kadloubovsky and G.E.H. Palmer, *Writings from the Philokalia on Prayer of the Heart* (London, 1951); but this should be employed with caution, for it is based, not directly on the Greek, but on Theophan's Russian version (often somewhat free). In French there is a succinct but excellent selection of sources, with good introductory notes, by Jean Gouillard, *Petite Philocalie de la Prière du Coeur* (Paris, 1953; reissued Paris, 1968).

(ii) Russian

Texts from Ignatius Brianchaninov and Theophan the Recluse (with some material from the Greek) are given by Igumen Chariton of Valamo, *The Art of Prayer: an Orthodox Anthology*, translated by E. Kadloubovsky and E.M. Palmer (London, 1966), pp. 75-123. See also Ignatius Brianchaninov, *On the Prayer of Jesus*, translated by Fr Lazarus (London, 1952; reissued London, 1965); and, by the same author and translator, *The Arena: an Offering to Contemporary Monasticism* (Madras, 1970; reissued Jordanville, New York, 1983), especially pp. 78-88. For a Western work, revised first by Nicodemus and then by Theophan, see *Unseen Warfare: being the Spiritual Combat and Path to Paradise of Lorenzo Scupoli as edited by Nicodemus of the Holy Mountain and revised by Theophan the Recluse*, translated by E. Kadloubovsky and G.E.H. Palmer (London, 1952); this has an interesting (but not always accurate) introduction by H.A. Hodges.

Practical Use

For advice on the practical use of the Jesus Prayer, by contemporary Orthodox authors, see first of all "A Monk of the Eastern Church" (Lev Gillet), *On the Invocation of the Name of Jesus* (The Fellowship of St Alban and St Sergius, London, 1950; reissued by SLG Press, Fairacres, Oxford, 1970): this is a fuller version of what appears as chapter VI in the present work. Consult also Tito Colliander, *The Way of the Ascetics* (London, 1960: new edition, London/Oxford, 1983), especially pp. 70-89, 107-12; Mother Maria, *The Jesus Prayer: the Meeting of East and West in the Prayer of the Heart* (Greek Orthodox Monastery of the Assumption, Filgrave [now at Normanby, N. Yorkshire], 1972); Archimandrite Sophrony, *His Life is Mine* (London/Oxford, 1977), pp. 99-128; Kallistos Ware, *The Power of the Name: The Jesus Prayer in Orthodox Spirituality* (Fairacres Publication 43: Oxford, 1974). For an appreciation of the Jesus Prayer by a Roman Catholic who lived in India, see Abhishiktananda (Henri le Saux, OSB, +1973), *Prayer* (3rd edition, London, 1974), pp. 51-58. Per-Olof Sjögren, *The Jesus Prayer* (London, 1975), provides a sympathetic treatment by a Swedish Lutheran.

The Physical Method

Much has been written—not all of it sober or exact—about the "physical" method of the Hesychasts and its apparent parallels in non-Christian religions. Those pursuing this fascinating question will do well to recall Fr Lev's clear insistence upon the distinctive character of the Jesus Prayer as an invocation addressed specifically to the person of Christ the Savior; they should keep in mind how he sets the Prayer firmly in the context of the Bible, the sacraments and the totality of the Christian life, and how he views the psychosomatic "technique" as no more than an accessory, perhaps useful to some but in no way essential. For a cautious interpretation of the physical "method", see Fr Anthony Bloom (now Metropolitan of Sourozh), *Asceticism (Somatopsychic techniques)* (The Guild of Pastoral Psychology, Guild Lecture 95: London, 1957). In his more recent writings, however—for example, in *Living Prayer* (London, 1966), pp. 84-88—Metropolitan Anthony only mentions the bodily techniques briefly, emphasizing the need here for "strict guidance by a spiritual father," and he prefers to concentrate upon the inner significance of the Prayer as expressing a personal relationship with Christ.

On the points of similarity—and also the significant differences—between Hindu and Hesychast techniques, see Jules Monchanin, "Yoga and Hesychasm," in *Cistercian Studies* 10, 2 (1975), pp. 85-92. Consult also Sister Vandana, *Nama Japa (The Prayer of the Name)* (Bombay, 1984). On the somewhat closer parallels in Sufism, see Louis Gardet, "Un problème de mystique comparée: la mention du nom divin (*dhikr*) dans la mystique musulmane," in *Revue Thomiste* 52 (1952), pp. 642-79; 53 (1953), pp. 197-216; reprinted in G.-C. Anawati and L. Gardet, *Mystique musulmane: aspects et tendances - expériences et techniques* (Paris, 1961), pp. 187-256. Compare also Jacques-Albert Cuttat, *The Encounter of Religions: A Dialogue between the West and the Orient, with an Essay on the Prayer of Jesus* (New York, 1960). The history of the prayer-rope or rosary is described by Eithne Wilkins, *The Rose-Garden Game. The symbolic background to the European prayer-beads* (London, 1969), but this tells us little about the Christian East.

Devotion to the Holy Name in the Christian West

A full study of this, by someone also familiar with the Orthodox tradition, is greatly needed. For the present, see A. Cabassut, "La dévotion au Nom de Jésus dans l'Eglise d'Occident," in *La View Spirituelle* 86 [369] (January 1952), pp. 46-69; Irénée Noye, "Jésus (Nom de)," in *Dictionnaire de Spiritualité* 8 (1974), cols. 1109-26; John A. Goodall, "The Invocation of the Name of Jesus in the English XIVth Century Spiritual Writers," in *Chrysostom* iii, 5

(1972), pp. 113-17; Kallistos Ware, "The Holy Name of Jesus in East and West: the Hesychasts and Richard Rolle," in *Sobornost incorporating Eastern Churches Review* iv, 2 (1982), pp. 163-84.

For more detailed bibliography, consult notes throughout this volume.

INDEX

119